In an age of religious fanaticism, an attitude of holy skepticism is no bad thing. This book stands in a fine tradition of radical Christian subversion—from Dante's *Divine Comedy* to Bono's spiritual quest—which has always sought to find and follow Jesus without kissing its brains good-bye. Wherever you're at on the journey of faith, I recommend this book to you as if it were a wise old companion whose conversation is warm, occasionally surprising and continually seasoned with the ancient convictions of orthodox faith.

Pete Greig
Co-founder, *24-7 Prayer*
Author, *The Vision and the Vow*

Larson and Mitchell have written a fresh and breezy introduction to basic Christianity. A nifty piece of work!

Rev. Cornelius Plantinga, Jr., Ph.D.
President and Professor of Systematic Theology,
Calvin Theological Seminary

a place for
SKEPTICS

SCOTT LARSON AND
CHRIS MITCHELL

Regal

From Gospel Light
Ventura, California, U.S.A.

Regal Books is a ministry of Gospel Light, a Christian publisher dedicated to serving the local church. We believe God's vision for Gospel Light is to provide church leaders with biblical, user-friendly materials that will help them evangelize, disciple and minister to children, youth and families.

Regal

It is our prayer that this Regal book will help you discover biblical truth for your own life and help you meet the needs of others. May God richly bless you.

For a free catalog of resources from Regal Books/Gospel Light, please call your Christian supplier or contact us at 1-800-4-GOSPEL *or* www.regalbooks.com.

Library of Congress Cataloging-in-Publication Data

Larson, Scott, 1959-
   A place for skeptics / Scott Larson, Chris Mitchell.
         p. cm.
   Includes bibliographical references.
   ISBN 0-8307-3705-7 (hard cover)
   1. Apostles' Creed. 2. Skepticism. 3. Belief and doubt. 4. Theology, Doctrinal. I. Mitchell, Chris, 1968- II. Title.
   BT993.3.L37 2005
   238'.11—dc22   2005014233

1   2   3   4   5   6   7   8   9   10   /   10   09   08   07   06   05

Rights for publishing this book in other languages are contracted by Gospel Light Worldwide, the international nonprofit ministry of Gospel Light. Gospel Light Worldwide also provides publishing and technical assistance to international publishers dedicated to producing Sunday School and Vacation Bible School curricula and books in the languages of the world. For additional information, visit www.gospellightworldwide.org; write to Gospel Light Worldwide, P.O. Box 3875, Ventura, CA 93006; or send an e-mail to info@gospellightworldwide.org

Foreword

I share a deep value with Chris Mitchell and Scott Larson. I believe that the good news of Jesus Christ is not intended for the religious only—or even primarily for them! I believe that it's intended for everyone, beginning with those who have never really understood the whole God-religion-church thing.

But if we're honest, especially as we look across the sweep of church history, we have to admit that the message of Jesus—intended especially for the irreligious—often is held hostage by the religious. Unintentionally, the religious develop insiders-only jargon that makes the message sound strange or distant. They may add to the message all kinds of cultural and cultic baggage. They may even declare "culture wars" against the irreligious and, instead of seeing them as beloved neighbors, see them as a threat to be overcome or a problem to be fixed. That's scary and sad and wrong.

So I feel a special kinship with people like Scott and Chris, because they're not going in that scary direction.

They're trying to translate the good news of Jesus Christ into language that anybody can understand. Instead of putting up walls, they're building bridges. Instead of making things sound complicated, they're making them clear. Instead of judging people or condemning them, they're making friends with them, listening to them and seeking to understand them, so they can serve them and help them.

That pretty much sums up the purpose of this book.

There's something else I have in common with Scott and Chris: they value the old creeds—like the Apostles' Creed. True, some people think the creeds are outdated and need to be jettisoned. But some of us think the creeds are like wine or friends or great art—and not like cars or computers or bread. The creeds appreciate with age; they distill seasoned, cherished, time-tested truth.

I love the old creeds for many reasons. They root us in the historic tradition of the church. They help us distinguish current fads from lasting essentials. But, as *A Place for Skeptics* makes clear, they also do something else very valuable and perhaps unexpected: They answer vital questions that we all face—questions about meaning, purpose, direction and hope for our lives. Chris and Scott make these answers available to anyone who has the curiosity to ask, whatever his or her religious (or nonreligious) background.

In the early centuries of the church, the creeds were used to help people new to Christian faith to understand the heart of the message—a message about God, about Jesus and about the Holy Spirit. In some ways, the creeds summarize a story that begins with God who creates and continues with God who intervenes and rescues and who can be experienced by people today. They remind us that the story isn't yet over. So they give us a past to remember, a present to seize and a future to reach toward.

Creeds don't tell us everything we'll ever need to know, but they're one of the best places to tell us what we need to know to get started. And that's quite a gift.

If you're just beginning to explore spirituality in general or Christian faith in particular, you've found a great book to help you take the next steps. If you're a ways down the road but would like a kind of check-up to be sure you have the basics down solid, you've got a great resource in your hands. And if you're already very knowledgeable about Christianity, maybe this book will help you to remember how to talk to people who aren't where you are. That's something you really should know, because then you can help Scott, Chris, me and all the other people like us who can't shake the feeling that Jesus' favorite people (if we can speak in terms of favorites) are not the ones who "get it" but rather are the ones who need it, want it and are seeking it. What is "it"? This book will help you discover that for yourself.

Brian McLaren
anewkindofchristian.com
crcc.org
emergentvillage.com

Before You Begin

If you have given up on church or traditional religion but not necessarily on God, this book was written with you in mind. It's an exploration of the questions, confusion and disappointment so many of us feel when it comes to God, and of how that affects our day-to-day lives.

To make your experience in reading this book as fulfilling as possible, we begin with a couple of suggestions.

First, there's no right way to read this book. While the reflections are anchored in the order and content of the Apostles' Creed, your reading of them doesn't need to be. How you read this book should start with who you are. What questions do you have? Which issues do you find most pressing at the moment? Just as a conversation with a friend can take many directions depending on the slice of life you're living in at the moment, these reflections are designed to speak to your current frame of mind. You can skip ahead, move around, start at the end. It really doesn't matter. Order is much less important than expectation.

Which takes us to the second suggestion:

If you are expecting a lot of answers, how-tos or formulas, this probably isn't the book for you. As a matter of fact, you may have *more* questions when you are finished than when you started.

In many ways, this book is more about asking good questions than delivering "right" answers. While finding answers is a reasonable goal when it comes to objective facts, the vast majority of life cannot be reduced to mere data. In areas like nurturing intimacy in our relationships or developing character, sitting on a good question can be of much greater benefit than trying to quickly seize on a handy answer.

A well-placed question provides a platform—an opening or a clearing—from which we can begin to see things from a whole different perspective. Rather than wallowing miserably in our pain or confusion, posing the right questions lifts us high enough to search the horizon for a glimpse of the bigger issues of life—issues that our current circumstances may bring to light. Questions help us consider how stepping into our problems rather than avoiding them might actually shape our future in brand-new ways.

So what qualifies as a good question? Generally a mind-opening question begins with the words "what," "how" and "where" versus "why." Questions like, Why is this happening to me? take up a lot of space in our lives and don't give much room for growth and change. But asking, "How am I responding to this situation, and what is the fruit of that?" opens up infinitely more possibilities for transformation.

Of course, asking these sorts of questions requires discipline and a willingness to look beneath the surface to find out what's at the heart of an issue: What is it about discussing religion and faith that gets me feeling so uptight? Or, How is the way I'm responding making things better or worse? And Where else is this pattern showing up in my life?

Choosing to look inward and daring to ask God to reveal a deeper truth as we elect to stay in the pain and discomfort a little longer unleashes the power of a good question.

Franciscan priest Richard Rohr says: "Religious energy is in the dark questions, seldom in the answers. Answers are the way out, but that is not what we are here for. . . . When we look at the questions, we see the opening to transformation. Fixing something doesn't usually transform us. We try to change events in order to avoid changing ourselves."[1]

That certainly describes our own experience in dodging the difficult questions; and with that in mind, we think of ourselves more as guides than experts in the area of wrestling with faith. An expert has a certain level of mastery in a particular field, while a guide is a fellow journeyer who's just a bit more familiar with the lay of the land. Experts work with facts and figures. Guides rely on landmarks, signs and their own previous experience and that of others.

Our words within this book draw on all these things and reflect the unique paths each of us has wandered with our questions. (The initials at the end of a reading indicate which of us wrote it.) We aren't claiming to offer much in the way of answers, but we'd like to point you toward some intriguing questions. If a particular topic resonates with where you are and you would like to delve into it more deeply, you'll notice that we recommend other books that expand on those themes in the footnotes.

So use this book as a guidebook. Dog-ear the pages. Tear out a reading or two to post where it will prompt you to think further on the questions raised. Use these words in whatever way they will help you think about God and wrestle with the issues that challenge your faith. Our hope is that this small volume might be one of many tools that you find useful on your journey with God. It might even be a tool that God uses on His journey with you.

Can Skepticism Be Spiritual?

Those who look for me find me.[2]

—GOD

Can someone with faith be a skeptic?

That depends on how you understand skepticism. Some people use the words "skepticism" and "cynicism" interchangeably. That doesn't work for us. We believe a certain amount of skepticism is good. Cynicism, however, is more like poison. Even a small amount can make you sick—if it doesn't kill you.

Cynics don't have room for doubt; they are committed to not believing. Skepticism, in contrast, is an attitude of closely examining something with the hope of believing. In fact, the dictionary defines skepticism as "a questioning attitude that believes inquiry must be a process of doubting in order to acquire approximate or relative certainty."[3] A skeptic may start from a point of doubt, but his or her objective is to examine the evidence thoroughly in search of truth. A skeptic may initially be unconvinced but still actively seeking truth. It's not that skeptics don't want to believe; in fact, they do. This is why you'll sometimes hear the phrase "healthy skepticism," but never "healthy cynicism."

We, too, want to believe, but we need good reasons and we like to use good reason. We also believe that when it comes to living a life of authentic faith, holy skepticism needs to be anchored in something beyond one's own experiences, which are restricted to a limited location at a particular point in time.

The Christian faith, while relevant to our context of time and space, is part of a much bigger story—a story that spans thousands of years and is filled with the written experiences of countless men and women from all over the world and from every era in history. When we consider how our story intersects with their stories, we're better able to connect with the story of God.

The Bible and the history of the Christian faith reveal the many facets of that story. But for this particular segment of the journey of faith, we have chosen to anchor our thoughts in the Apostles' Creed.

"Why the Apostles' Creed?" you might ask. At first glance it doesn't get us terribly excited either. As children, we both attended churches where the Apostles' Creed was read weekly. And while the words still come back when prompted—sort of like the spontaneous finishing of the first few words of a familiar jingle from childhood—in our early encounters with the Creed the words seemed to lack any significance or relevance to real life.

So why are we suggesting that you bind the next several days of your life to this old and antiquated confession?

While some churches have trivialized the Apostles' Creed to a level of empty or rote dogma, that is certainly not the attitude of those who initially penned or used it. That early band of Christ followers back in the first century lived amidst a plethora of differing and competing ideologies that offered a precarious basis upon which to build a life of authentic faith. In other words, they had a lot in common with those of us who desire to better know and serve God in the twenty-first century.

No doubt those early church leaders found it somewhat frustrating that Jesus had seemingly given little thought to organizational structure. Nor did He condense the heart of His teaching into any single concise verbal formula for His followers to build upon. We, like those followers of old, would probably prefer more concrete instructions on what to do in individual situations. Instead we're left with the eternal riddles of whether Jesus would drive an SUV, eat meat, put His kids in public schools . . . the list goes on.

The Apostles' Creed doesn't get that specific, but its writers did outline a set of fundamental beliefs to help govern the actions of all who would choose to follow the teachings of Christianity while walking in a world of competing values and ideals. For emerging generations who lacked the firsthand encounter with Jesus and the launching of His church, the Creed provided a broad yet concise understanding of the essence of Christ—what He was about and what it means to throw one's faith on Him.

In a nutshell, the Apostles' Creed is the most succinct, most universal, and most ancient celebration of faith in the church today. And we believe you will find that rather than being a distant document, it actually hits quite close to where you live. It was born in the hearts and minds of men and women who loved their families, worked hard and desired a life of meaning and purpose—just as you do. They feared disease, divorce and depression. But they feared in faith. And this Creed outlines the bedrock of their faith.

In many ways the Creed has become the story of our faith too. We can't say that we understand it all. We can't say that it answers every question we have about life, about God, or even about ourselves. But it has become a story that makes a difference on the

Monday morning commute, when we're answering e-mails and voice mails, and when we're reading bedtime stories to our children.

The reason? Rather than something we simply mumble in unison with our fellow skeptics, the Apostles' Creed contains real-life answers to real-life questions. It helps us begin to wrap our head and heart around the God who is our Father, our Creator, our friend, master, teacher, advocate, lover, judge and coworker.

Of course, to succeed in the search for unshakeable faith, we need the rest of Scripture as well as the companionship of fellow journeyers and the reflection of all that we've experienced in life. But like those early followers of Jesus, the Creed helps us skeptics to organize the right questions.

Ultimately the path we will tread together for the next several days is a journey toward faith. Whether faith seems to you a nebulous concept or a lifeline you'd desperately like to grab hold of, we encourage you to continue on, with both your skeptical questions and your desire to believe at the ready.

You can trust the words of Jesus when He said, "Ask and you'll get; Seek and you'll find; Knock and the door will open. Don't bargain with God. Be direct. Ask for what you need. This is not a cat-and-mouse, hide-and-seek game we're in."[4]

Jesus has declared that God wants to be found, that He wants us to experience a deeper and more meaningful relationship with Him. He's even promised that we will find Him, if we look. The ball's in our court.—*SL & CM*

A Conversation with God

Dear God, sometimes I'm not altogether sure what I believe or why I believe it. But I do want to know you. I want to find you. I thank you that you're walking with me on this journey, even though it often doesn't feel like it. I invite you to play an even bigger role: Guide me, lead me, help me, God. I want to rest in you. I want to work with you.

Making It Real

Would you consider yourself primarily a cynic or a skeptic? Explain your answer.

Write out and post these questions somewhere to reflect on today: Do I really want to find God? and Where am I looking? Allow these questions to prompt you to consider the posture of your mind and heart as you face different ideas and thoughts in your search.

For Further Exploration

An interesting series of letters between a son and his agnostic father regarding issues of faith can be found in Gregory and Edward Boyd's *Letters from a Skeptic: A Son Wrestles with His Father's Questions About Christianity* (Wheaton, IL: Victor Books, 1994).

The **Apostles'** Creed

I believe in God, the Father almighty,
    creator of heaven and earth.
I believe in Jesus Christ, his only Son, our Lord,
    who was conceived by the Holy Spirit
    and born of the virgin Mary.
    He suffered under Pontius Pilate,
    was crucified, died, and was buried;
    he descended to hell.
    The third day he rose again from the dead.
    He ascended to heaven
    and is seated at the right hand of God the Father
        almighty.
    From there he will come to judge the living and
the dead.
I believe in the Holy Spirit,
    the holy catholic church,
    the communion of saints,
    the forgiveness of sins,
    the resurrection of the body,
    and the life everlasting, Amen.[5]

Who Really Believes This Stuff?

Consider carefully what you hear. With the measure you use, it will be measured to you—and even more.[6]

—JESUS

Our personal creed begins with who we are, what we've experienced and how we've chosen to process those experiences. Likewise, the Apostles' Creed begins with all that is buried in the simple one-letter word: *I.*

I remember walking down the street with a young person who recently had been released from lock-up. Wanting to illustrate healthy, positive behavior at every opportunity, I pointed to a teenager holding an elderly woman's arm as they crossed the street.

"Isn't it nice how that young man is helping that woman cross a dangerous street?" I remarked.

My companion looked at the same scene and said, "Somebody should warn her to hold on tight to her purse. That kid's just found an easy target."

We didn't stick around long enough to see which of us had the more accurate interpretation of the scene, but clearly we were viewing it through vastly different lenses.

In the verse that opens this chapter, Jesus admonished His followers to consider carefully what they saw and heard—in essence, to notice what they were looking and listening for. Why? Because we tend to see what we're looking for. Whatever we train our ears to be alert for is what we ultimately hear and act upon. Perhaps that seems to be an obvious truth, but consider the implications: What questions serve as the filter for your response? What do you naturally listen for in conversation?

Can this person be trusted?

Does what he is saying fit with what I believe?

What's not working here, and how can I fix it?

Does this person approve of me or not?

How can I best get my point across?

What's *not* being said?

How can I respond in a way that will make me look good?

The way we listen to what's being said wields as much power as—if not more than—the words actually being expressed.

Jesus also said that what we hear or listen for is what we ultimately end up with. Have you ever noticed how many of your thoughts become self-fulfilling prophecies? When you're concerned about someone's trustworthiness, he or she inevitably displays actions that confirm your suspicions. You get what you're looking for.

Our ways of hearing, seeing and thinking become the filters through which we experience life. In other words, every act of listening contains two distinct conversations: what you are saying and what I am telling myself *about* what you are saying. It is the latter conversation that most influences my response. Father Anthony De Mello from India said it this way: "You see persons and things not as they are but as you are."[7]

Another way to describe these filters is with the term "creeds." While the word "creed" may conjure up images of ancient documents, a creed is simply a set of fundamental beliefs that govern our actions. By that definition, we all have creeds.

Perhaps you've noticed a few of the following creeds while careening down the highway at 65 mph or so:

"Whoever dies with the most toys wins."

"Life sucks, and then you die."

"Jesus is coming. Look busy."

Cemeteries are a good place to stroll for a more solemn type of creed. In an old Boston graveyard, I saw a sobering inscription on a gravestone dating to the early 1700s:

Stand here a minute and cast an eye.

As you are now, so once was I.

As I am now, soon you will be.

Prepare to die and follow me.

Creeds serve to anchor our thoughts and our hearing on something outside ourselves. If you're open to considering the notion that you, too, have a creed that governs your actions, then it merits some reflection on just what that creed is.

In other words, where does your faith come from? What do you believe? And possibly the most demanding question of all: why?

Inherent to all faith is the recognition of its object—that thing in which we believe and trust. Sometimes that thing comes from reliable, trustworthy and helpful places (such as men and women with wisdom and experience) or from time-tested principles. Other times faith is simply formed in and through superstition or rote tradition.

What is it about the object of your faith—your deepest convictions about life, death, God, the universe or whatever guides you in your everyday drive to work as you answer voice mails and e-mails and put your kids to bed—that is so believable? These are not easy questions to ask, let alone answer. And some of the answers come only in pieces.

The apostle Paul demonstrated the immense im-pact of one's personal creed. He had enjoyed plenty of notoriety when he was persecuting Christians, but after he decided to follow Christ, he spent a good deal of time in prison and endured a myriad of other forms of persecution as well. Doesn't sound like a very good deal, does it?

Yet through Paul's letters we gain a glimpse of his creed and how it shaped his response to life. Something he wrote in his letter from prison to the Philippian Christians captures it well: "For to me, to live is Christ and to die is gain."[8]

Paul obviously knew the truth that while we can't control what happens to us, we can control how we interpret and respond to our circumstances. Living in a creed that we deem worthy of our lives can actually alter the way we hear. Had the apostle Paul interpreted his imprisonment in a more natural way, he would have invested his energies in writing petitions for his release rather than penning half of the New Testament Scriptures.

Notice how he saw, heard and interpreted his prison experience:

> I want to report to you, friends, that my imprisonment here has had the opposite of its intended effect. Instead of being squelched, the Message has actually prospered. All the soldiers here, and everyone else too, found out that I'm in jail because of this Messiah. That piqued their curiosity, and now they've learned all about him. Not only that, but most of the Christian here have become far more sure of themselves in the faith than ever, speaking out fearlessly about God, about the Messiah.[9]

We all make commitments to creeds, whether consciously or subconsciously. But more important, those commitments ultimately make us. Spend a moment today considering the creed that is shaping your life.—*SL*

A Conversation with God

God, reveal to me what I'm listening and living for.
Show me how my filters have shaped my response to
life and those around me. Expand my mind to

embrace a bigger creed, one that includes you and is
worthy of giving my whole life to.

Making It Real

Honestly consider what filters are at work in your life. What do you naturally listen for, and how does this shape your interpretation of what's happening? Some examples might include: the need to look good, to feel good, to be right or to be in control.

If your best friend were to describe the creed you live by, what do you think he or she would say?

Write a creed that would be worth giving your life to.

On a scale of 1 to 10, with 10 being right on target, how would you rate your effectiveness in following that creed?

For Further Exploration

An excellent book for those who may have given up on church and religious creeds but not on God and spirituality is Brian McLaren's *A New Kind of Christian: A Tale of Two Friends on a Spiritual Journey* (San Francisco: Jossey-Bass, 2001).

What About When Doubt Overshadows Belief?

I believe . . .

I do believe; help me overcome my unbelief! [10]

—A FATHER CONVERSING WITH JESUS ABOUT HIS SON
IN NEED OF HEALING

My wife and I recently took a big step of faith. We believed that God wanted the organization that we direct, Straight Ahead Ministries, to build a 24-bed residential school and vocational training program for kids coming out of juvenile detention centers. Shortly after we began talking about it, a camp approached us and offered to donate five acres of land surrounded by a beautiful state forest. We thanked God for what we perceived as His obvious role in opening door after door to bring us closer to the goal.

Then, those doors began slamming shut. One beautiful Saturday afternoon our family drove through the community to look for a potential new home. My nine-year-old daughter was the first to notice the signs posted everywhere. Most simply read: "STOP THE PRISON!" But others were more expressive: "WE CAME HERE TO BUY OUR PIECE OF HEAVEN, AND HELL IS STRAIGHT AHEAD MINISTRIES!"

"Dad, I don't want to move here," said my eight-year-old son, David. "These people don't want us, and I'd be afraid I'd get beat up if I went to school here."

"Don't worry, David," I assured him. "God is leading us in this, and we just need to believe that He will turn it around." That assertion seemed to satisfy my son for the moment.

But rather than following through on that anticipated U-turn, things proceeded directly from bad to worse. After receiving a few death threats, spending thousands of dollars on endangered species and traffic studies, and enduring months of opposition from town officials and citizens, my own faith started taking the hit. Even at the moment of this writing, I have no clear sense if this project will ever be completed.

Meanwhile, my questions far outnumber any answers I've received. Early questions like, God, where are you in all of this? gradually gave way to, God, did you really speak to me at all, or was it just my own ideas and desires being wrongly attributed to you? And then, questions like, Do you really speak to and lead people at all, God? eventually led to, Do you even exist?

My faith and belief in God is emerging out of the mire of this ordeal, but it's emerging differently—in many ways stronger, but certainly different.

Here are some of the things I'm learning about what it means to believe in God.

1. Belief Requires Trust

Believing *in* God is quite different from believing God. Eighty-five percent of Americans claim to believe in God, but very few of us really reorient our lives around that belief.[11] It seems that we aren't willing to place our trust in our beliefs.

Augustus Gordon is a modern-day monk who spends one-half of his year in solitude, seclusion and prayer and the other half ministering to the poor in Haiti, Jamaica and other Caribbean islands. When asked if he could define the Christian life in a single sentence, he didn't blink an eye. He said, "I can define it in a single word—trust."[12]

The apparent quagmire of our ministry project has revealed to me just how much I detest having to trust someone else, even—or perhaps especially—when that someone is God. I want certainty and clarity; I don't want to live by faith.

Could it be that my goals run counter to those of God? The Bible says, "We live by faith, not by sight"[13] and, "Faith is being sure of what we hope for and certain of what we do *not* see."[14] While I'm seeking every opportunity to avoid the risk of trusting in God, He's actually giving me opportunities to demonstrate trust.

It reminds me of the man who traveled around the world to meet with Mother Teresa and ask her to pray for him. When she asked what he wanted prayer for, he replied, "Pray that I have clarity."

"No, I will not do that!" Mother Teresa quickly responded. "Clarity is the last thing you are clinging to and must let go of." When he noted that she always seemed to have the clarity he longed for, she laughed and said, "I have never had clarity; what I have always had is trust. So I will pray that you trust God."[15]

2. Belief Is Not the Absence of Doubt

Of the more than 200 references to "trust" in the Bible, the vast majority of these appear in the Psalms, where trust is tested over and over.

Most of the psalms open with the writer candidly voicing confusion, doubt and despair. Then he reviews what he has experienced to be true about God in the past. Finally, he concludes once more that God can be trusted during this confusing time as well. Seldom has the situation changed before the writer comes to this verdict. Thankfully, God has allowed us to eavesdrop on the whole process and not just how it turned out.

The psalmist's anguished words reveal that trust is not the absence of doubt. Rather, trust is most often deepened by working through the presence of doubt. As the Russian novelist Fyodor Dostoevsky so profoundly said, "Sometimes the greatest act of faith is in the doubting." In my own life, God is not answering all of my questions or even changing the circumstances, but He is becoming more real to me as I dare to honestly engage Him with my doubts, fears and disappointments.

3. Belief Demands Action

In Hebrew thinking, the perspective dominant among the biblical writers and prophets was that a belief was not a belief until it was acted on. On the other hand, Greek philosophy tended to distance belief from action. This viewpoint led to dualism—a perceived separation between the material and spiritual aspects of life—which still pervades much of contemporary thought.

However you define trust or belief, one thing is certain: It requires action on our part if it is to grow. Jonathan Edwards, an eighteenth-century theologian and scholar, once said, "You can always tell what a person really believes by his or her actions." In other words, regardless of what we may say, we always act on our strongest belief.

This, of course, exposes the reality that we often entertain conflicting beliefs at the same time. I may say that I believe God is in control and will meet all my needs. But if I spend more time worrying about things than praying about them, my actions reveal a stronger belief that my success and security rest entirely with me. Worry, then, is the warning light that I'm trusting in something other than God.

The Latin word for anxiety is *angustia*, which literally means "narrowness."[16] It seems that every time I attempt to fit God and His ways into the small and narrow box of how I think things ought to be, the result is anxiety and doubt. But I've learned that when I authentically confess my doubts before Him, faith begins to emerge right alongside those doubts. And in time a new and greater belief that is anchored in who God really is breaks out of that puny little box, shattering the narrowness of my doubts.—*SL*

A Conversation with God

*Dear God, I do believe. But help me overcome my
unbelief. I want to trust you more, believing that you
truly do have my best interests at heart. I know
many things are holding me back. Please reveal them
to me one by one and peel off those layers of self-
protection with which I've learned to cloak myself.*

Making It Real

Jot down some of the things that you think might be
holding you back from trusting God more fully. For
example, bad experiences in church, hurts that you
believe God could have or should have prevented, mysteries regarding the intersection between science and
the supernatural or areas of your life that you fear sur-
rendering to God. Present these to God one at a time,
confessing the fears that feed your doubts, and ask
Him to give you the strength and courage to trust Him
with each.

For Further Exploration

For more on what it means to trust God, consider
reading Brennan Manning's book *Ruthless Trust: The
Ragamuffin's Path to God* (San Francisco: HarperSan-
Francisco, 2002). █

Do You Ever Wonder About God?

> *So who even comes close to being like God? To whom or what can you compare him? . . . GOD doesn't come and go. God lasts. He's Creator of all you can see or imagine. He doesn't get tired out, doesn't pause to catch his breath. And he knows everything, inside and out.*[17]

—THE PROPHET ISAIAH

My first trip to the Grand Canyon and Lake Powell served as an awakening of sorts. I had seen the pictures. I had read the articles. But actually being there and *experiencing* these massive, breathtaking sights was altogether different. All the colors and shapes, heights and depths exceeded my ability to absorb and take them in. It was all so much bigger than I had imagined, so much bigger than me. I was filled with wonder.

When were you last struck by the knowledge of something immensely bigger than you, something truly *wonder*-ful? A newborn baby, tiny though she may be, can fill adults with wonder and awe. A clean bill of health after a bout with cancer can render you speechless. Watching a lightning storm from the top of a mountain can also fill you with wonder, along with a little fear.

Sometimes after an experience of wonder, people say, "I'll never be the same." Such encounters with the vast mysteries of life can transform our perspectives.

Has the thought of God ever filled you with wonder? Think, for a moment, about how "big" He is, beyond our ability to absorb or comprehend. The Apostles' Creed leads us into a story of a God who is not only big, but who is also beyond everything—*wonder*-ful. Even if you are a skeptic and your faith is tenuous at best, that little shred of faith, amidst all your doubts, still points to *God*.

Let this sink in. Don't skip over the immensity of this truth, for that would be like peeking at the Grand Canyon for a second and saying, "Oh, that's nice. Can we get some lunch?"

Just look at that word "God" for a minute. He has no beginning. He has no end. He makes *things* out of no-*thing*. He knows absolutely everything there is to know. He thought it all up in the first place! He is beyond both space and time. The *God*-ness of God is a mind-bending concept. He transcends all of our human categories, limits and boundaries. He is a big God, to say the least.

Americans are known for liking big things. Our cars, meals and homes are all pretty big compared to those found in most cultures. It's ironic then that so often our concept of God isn't very big at all. We've reduced the "Creator of all" to the "man upstairs"—someone understandable, explainable. No wonder we've lost our sense of wonder about God.

I'm sure we have lots of reasons for trying to shrink God down to a manageable size. We like control. We fear surrender. We crave certainty. Sometimes we're so busy trying to run the world ourselves that we overlook the opportunities we have to see and remember just how big God is. Whatever the reason, when we shrink God, the result isn't just less wonder, it's less life.

Consider what happens when we allow ourselves to revel in amazement at the mysteries of life, such as babies and good health and a lightning storm. These things don't shrink us; they expand us. In some powerful and mysterious way, things that are much more wonderful than ourselves connect us to their wonder. So, just imagine how our lives are enhanced when we have a real encounter with God. Saint Augustine, one of the most brilliant theologians in the history of Christianity, simply concluded, "God is best known in wonder."

So do you want a God you can control, or do you want to connect to a God who is bigger than us, even bigger than life? Your life will answer that question.—*CM*

A Conversation with God

Dear God, I'm starting to understand that I will never really "get" you. I am a creature; you are the Creator. I am a human; you are God. I recognize that I still have yet to know the vast majority of you. But I want to know more of you. And I thank you that in your vastness you are not completely beyond me. I ask you to show me your wonder—in creation, in Scripture, and in my family, my friends, my work and my play. I am looking for you, God. Show yourself to me gently. I want my faith to be stretched, to be clarified, to be humbled. Help me to find you.

Making It Real

Take out your date book and set aside a 15-minute time slot this week to get alone and think. When the time comes, write out the symbol for infinity (∞). Wonder about infinity—forever, endlessness—as a characteristic of God. After thinking this through for a few minutes, go someplace where you can look at the sky. Imagine God filling it as far as your mind can stretch. Now imagine Him also filling you. Each time you look at the sky for the rest of the week, remember that He is God, He is infinite—and bask in the wonder of that truth.

For Further Exploration

For a fresh perspective on the topic of seeing God in wonder, read Mike Yaconelli's *Dangerous Wonder* (Colorado Springs, CO: NavPress, 2003). ▪

Is *Father* Really the Best Word to Describe God?

I believe in God, **the Father . . .**

> *This, then, is how you should pray, "Our father in heaven . . ."* [18]

—JESUS, TEACHING HIS FOLLOWERS HOW TO PRAY

I was only 13 years old at the time, but the memory is as clear as if it happened yesterday. Our neighbor had asked my father if he and I could join several others in our rural community to help him load several thousand turkeys to bring to market on Thursday night.

Our neighborhood was known for coming together to help those in need, but personally I was motivated by the promise of being paid for my services. That $150 would give me just enough money to buy the motorcycle I'd been saving up for, making the dismal prospect of hacking turkey feathers all day seem worthwhile.

We ended up pulling an all-nighter, after which I quickly showered and headed off to school. Later that day, when my dad returned home from work, I was anxious to collect the cash that I was sure he was holding. "Oh, he didn't give me the money yet. He'll probably send a check in the mail."

I monitored the mail every day for the next week—and pestered my dad just as often about where the money was. "Don't worry, I'm sure he'll get it to us," was his only response.

After several weeks it became clear to me that we had been "played." Though I pleaded with my dad to go settle up with the neighbor, he never did.

I remember privately vowing at age 13 that I would never let myself be played as my father had—a vow that fed my anger toward many people over the years.

Not only did that event influence my future response in other situations, but it also significantly shaped my view of my father—and consequently my view of God. While I've never questioned my father's love for me, I did question his ability, or moxie, to deal effectively with tough situations. Similarly, my mental picture of God suggests a nice guy who is rather passive in how He engages in life. Over the years, my experience of God has actually proven this untrue in many instances, yet it continues to be my first response when trouble or hard times come my way. Whenever things get tough, I tend to navigate by the belief that if anything of significance is going to happen it will be up to me.

Chris, my coauthor, and I recently were talking about how our dads helped shape our view of God. The subject came up when he remarked at how "leaveable" he often feels when thinking about his family and friends. I thought it to be a strange and unfounded feeling for someone as gifted and engaging as I know Chris to be. But when he shared about how his own biological father had abandoned him and his mother while Chris was still in the womb, it made more sense. Although his mother later married a man who stepped in to take on the role of his father, that early experience left an indelible mark on Chris's life.

Mothers also wield significant influence over a child's image of God. But for whatever reason, it seems that absent or abusive fathers tend to be much more prevalent than destructive or disengaged moms.

I remember being approached by a 16-year-old boy named Ricky after I wrapped up my first speaking session at a weekend retreat for high schoolers. "I just hope you're not heading down a path where at the end of the weekend you're going to ask us to make some kind of commitment to follow God with our whole lives," he said, "'Cause if you are, I want to go home right now."

Without pausing for breath, Ricky continued: "I've been coming here for a long time, and I've made these promises year after year—promises I can never keep—and then I end up worse off than before I started, with God even more mad at me. 'Cause now, not only am I sinning, but I'm breaking another promise I made to Him. And so I just want to make sure that's not where you're headed this weekend. Is it?"

Feeling sad for Ricky and not knowing exactly how to respond to him, I took a shot in the dark and asked: "What can you tell me about your dad, Ricky?"

He proceeded to tell me a story from when he was in the fifth grade. "Every day when my dad came home from work, the first thing he would always ask me was, 'Have you done your homework yet?' It was a pretty safe bet that I hadn't.

"Then one day I decided to surprise him. When he got home, I met him at the door saying, 'Guess what, Dad. I did all my homework!'

"His response was, 'Then why aren't you working on tomorrow's?'"

Suddenly it wasn't so surprising that Ricky felt the way he did about himself and about God. He had learned that no matter how close he came, the mark of approval would always move a few notches higher. He would always come up short.

This subconscious act of transferring the flaws of our own parents to God's image is a scary thought, especially now that I have children of my own. No father I know can possibly reflect what God is really like. But the concept of God as a parent can also shed some light on His character. By considering how I see my own children and love them, I think I've gained a better understanding of how God views me. Jesus said, "If your child asks for bread, do you trick him with sawdust? If he asks for fish, do you scare him with a live snake on his plate? As bad as you are, you wouldn't think of such a thing. You're at least decent to your own children. So don't you think the God who conceived you in love will be even better?"[19]

So what is the heavenly Father really like? In Luke 15:11-32, we find one of the best known portraits of God, drawn by Jesus, in the story we have come to know as "The Prodigal Son." Perhaps it might better be titled *The Outrageously Loving Dad*.

Rather than preparing an "I told you so" lecture, the father ran down the road to meet his wayward child—the very one who had completely disappeared without so much as a "thank you" after demanding his share of the family fortune. The one who had squandered his half of the family assets and in the process cut his father's earning ability in half. The one who had wasted all that hard-earned money on sex, drugs and wild parties. The one who had treated his father as expendable—until there was nowhere else to turn.

It was this scandal-plagued child that the father ran out to meet, threw his arms around and kissed. Filled with compassion, the father ordered his servants to bring the best robe to his son, to put a ring on his finger and sandals on his feet, and then to bring the fattened calf and prepare a feast. Here was cause for celebration: His son who was lost was now found!

Believe it or not, that's exactly the way God—your divine Dad—feels about you. Are you ready to set aside your misconceptions and relate to Him on that level?—*SL*

A Conversation with God

Dear Dad . . . I must admit it sounds awkward to call you Dad. But it also blows me away that you would invite me to. I wonder how things might change if I really understood you as my loving father. Reveal more of that understanding to me, Father, so that I can trust you more, as a child trusts a loving parent.

Making It Real

Imagine that you are God—the heavenly Father—gazing at you and the circumstances in your life, longing to meet you there in the same way that you would want to connect with your own child. What would you say? Would your father God be any less compassionate?

Think back on your childhood to find one pivotal moment that captures your father or mother's parenting style or relationship with you. How has that image colored your view of God?

For Further Exploration

Incredible insights on the prodigal son and how God sees us as His children can be found in Henri J. M. Nouwen's *The Return of the Prodigal Son* (New York: Doubleday, 1992). ▨

What Good Is a God Who Doesn't Show Up When You Need Him?

I believe in God, the Father **almighty** . . .

Let's see if Elijah comes to take him down.[20]

—AN ONLOOKER MOCKING JESUS AS HE HUNG ON THE CROSS

I watched with amusement as my son, with a towel pinned around his neck like a cape, stretched out his arms and pointed his hands ahead of him. Making swooshing noises, he sped through the house—faster than a speeding bullet, more powerful than a locomotive, able to leap sofa cushions in a single bound. He was Superman.

Something inside each of us longs to be invincible. We want bullets to bounce off our chest. We want to fly over traffic jams. We want bad people to cower in fear at the mere mention of our name. Even if we don't want superpowers for ourselves, we at least want someone else who will be all that for us. Being a hero makes us feel powerful; having a hero makes us feel secure.

For the most part, we age our way beyond our superhero dreams. But when we're assaulted by life, we're quick to call on the ultimate superhero—God.

Okay, God, Mom is sick. This is where You swoop down and heal her.

Okay, God, this is my seventh month of unemployment. This is when You fly by and drop a job in my lap.

Okay, God, this is when You flex your divine muscles and show me how strong you are. You are God almighty, right?

We're used to movies and books and comic strips where the superhero flies in, flexes his muscles and decimates the bad guys in one fell swoop. But God rarely does anything of the sort. It's almost as if He's reading from a different script than we are.

He's definitely a different kind of hero. He doesn't swoop down to snatch us out of harm's way like Superman or swing by to dispatch trouble like Spiderman. He is the God-man who came to earth in the form of a baby and spent His first year learning how to crawl. Not exactly the kind of almighty hero we may have in mind.

Does that mean God is weak? No. He is, according to the Bible, the most powerful being of all, the sole creator, sustainer and redeemer of the cosmos. Yet He often chooses to show His strength in and through weakness. This is hinted at right in one of God's most familiar titles in Scripture found in Isaiah 9:6: That title is "Mighty God." In Aramaic, one basic meaning of the word "mighty" is "to restore, to raise up, or to rise."[21] Thus, contained in the title Mighty God is the process of *re*building. In other words, He is not just a powerful creator, but he also the master re-creator, the king of restoration. His power is displayed not through brute strength but through His ability to rebuild what has been torn down, heal what has been broken and reconcile what has been ripped apart.

It's when we have ruined something that we are most open to having someone restore it. It's in our losses, our pain, our most difficult experiences that we are most likely to ask for help. God's strength is at its peak when it works in and through our weakness. And the more honest we choose to be about the depth of our weakness, the more likely we are to look to God. I think it's what the apostle Paul was getting at when he said, "When I am weak, then I am strong—the less I have the more I depend on him."[22]

My friend Dana's mother was diagnosed with multiple sclerosis (MS) when he was 12.

Some have likened this disease to watching the hour hand of a clock. It moves so slowly you can't see it, yet every time you remember to look back at it, it has jumped farther ahead. That's the way MS kills—slowly, steadily, consistently and relentlessly bringing one closer and closer to death's door.

By the time Dana turned 40, this chronic degenerative disease had made a spectacle out of his mother's weakness. Her final five years were the worst. Things eventually got so bad that his mother had to be moved to the hospital.

Describing his sense of discouragement, Dana said, "Near the end, it seemed like we lost—like MS won. It seemed that all our efforts had added nothing. But then I realized that there was one thing this disease couldn't kill: my love for my mom. As a matter of fact, the weaker she grew, the more I loved her. MS couldn't take that, it couldn't stop it, it couldn't even touch it."

And then he said, "For me, when I look at the Cross—the ultimate place of weakness, pain and vulnerability—I know that it's there that real strength, ultimate power and true love is strengthened and forged."

Dana has learned that it's in our greatest weakness that God's love for us, His love in us, and His love through us is truly almighty.

Which leaves us with a different kind of superhero. One who doesn't always choose to rescue us from every troubling circumstance, but instead walks through them alongside us, lending us His strength and in the process restoring wholeness to lives that have been fractured.

Last week, as our family was watching the movie *Spiderman,* my eight-year-old son remarked, "Wouldn't it be cool to have those kinds of powers?"

Yeah, it would be cool. But it's nothing compared to the power of a God who can turn weakness on its head, who not only can meet us at our lowest points—in our weakest moments—but who *wants* to bring us strength from it.

He's not some heavenly superhero; He is God the Father almighty.—CM

A Conversation with God

Dear Father almighty, sometimes I want you to be a hero for me, on my terms. But that doesn't seem to be how you work. I want to know what it means that you are almighty, that you are strong in weakness, that you are able to suffer with me and for me. God almighty, help me to trust in your power. Grow my patience; help me to wait for your timing. Grow my faith; help me to see the beauty of your strength in and through my weakness.

Making It Real

Name one area of your life where you feel particularly weak—perhaps in a certain relationship or in a habit or vice in which you feel as if you are failing at times. Make this weakness a place to start rebuilding, to start restoring. Let this be the place and time to follow God almighty and to start rebuilding. What specific next step will you take right now to begin anew?

For Further Exploration

Two great books on finding God's presence and power in the midst of life's greatest difficulties are Philip Yancey's *Where Is God When It Hurts?* (Grand Rapids, MI: Zondervan Publishing House, 2001) and Larry Crabb's *Finding God* (Grand Rapids, MI: Zondervan Publishing House, 1993).

What Was God Thinking When He Created People?

. . . creator of heaven and earth . . .

*Let us make human beings in our image,
make them reflecting our nature.*[23]

—GOD

One Halloween my friends and I were out enjoying the wonder of filling a pillowcase with gum and Snickers and whatever else we could get our little hands on. As we were finishing our door-to-door ritual, one of my friends started screaming and running. A big dark shadow was chasing him. Then, from every direction, more dark shadows emerged. The rest of us started running, our hearts lodged in the back of our throats.

It turned out that one of my friend's older brother, along with a few accomplices, had decided to seize the opportunity to scare the crap out of us.

But that's not all they did. They also sprayed us with something. At first I thought it was water, but while we were huffing and puffing our way toward the safety of home, something started to reek. It smelled like urine, which in fact it was. They had sprayed us with deer urine, the kind used by hunters. Talk about a nasty trick. What began as a fun annual ritual with my buddies left me feeling humiliated, even violated.

Have you ever felt like that? Maybe someone vandalized your car, your locker at school, or your home. Having someone destroy something you value is an ugly experience, one that leaves a lasting impression.

One reason that vandalism cuts so deep is that it goes against our very nature. Human beings are created in God's image, and He is a creator, not a destroyer. He made us—actually designed us—to be like Him. We were created to create, not to destroy one another or this Earth He entrusted to us:

God created human beings; he created them godlike, reflecting God's nature. He created them male and female. God blessed them: "Prosper! Reproduce! Fill Earth! Take charge! Be responsible for fish in the sea and birds in the air, for every living thing that moves on the face of Earth." God looked over everything he had made; it was so good, so very good![24]

Most people, if they believe in God at all, seem to have no problem accepting God as the Creator. It seems logical that if there is a God, He probably made everything. Still, conversations about creation can easily get tangled in endless discussions about exactly *how* or *when* God created humanity. But for me, this overshadows the far more important question of *why*. Living with an understanding of my purpose on Earth seems to me not only a good idea, but an essential one. And according to the Bible verses above, one of our primary purposes is to serve as reflections of His image here on Earth.

The concept of imaging and reflecting another's nature is most clearly illustrated in the way children tend to reflect their parents. People often remark on how my children resemble me in appearance; but the similarities extend far beyond that. My children reflect me in both the characteristics that date back to my own childhood and in the behaviors that I've developed as an adult. When one of my daughters does her math homework with one hand—seven minutes before school—while eating breakfast with the other hand, she is reflecting both my tendency to procrastinate and my ability to multitask. And when another daughter checks her hair and clothing to be sure that everything is in place and looks just right before she walks out the door, she is imaging my own personal habits.

Whereas we as parents provide imperfect images that our children accurately reflect (to our occasional horror), God bestowed on us His perfect nature, which we have corrupted and warped.

Think about the notion of our being created to create. And then think about the devastation that happens when we instead allow ourselves to become fundamentally consumers and devourers.

If imaging God means we will prosper, multiply or increase, what happens when we instead see the world as something to consume? [25] Rather than enriching God's creation, we strip it. Instead of making it more beautiful, we make it less so. First we become consumers and devourers; then we become vandals. And in the process we violate the very core of who we are.

Stop and think about this for a minute. What would your life look like if you approached it asking questions like these:

Since I am made in the image of God, what good things can I create within the context of my career?

Since I am created in the image of God, how will I care for my home, my body?

Since I am created in the image of God, how will I use my gifts, my experiences, my time, my money?

Since I am created in the image of God, what kind of friend, spouse or parent will I be?

As you allow these questions to guide your daily choices, who knows? Someone might even say something like, "You looked just like *your Father* when you did that." Not only is it possible, but it is one of the reasons He made us in the first place.—*CM*

A Conversation with God

Dear Father, creator God, you have made me.
I don't want to take that simple fact for granted today. You made the world and everything in it.
And you continue to create things new even today.
I am created to create, Father. Help me today to see the opportunities you give me for creating good things. Please show me—at work, at home, with friends and with family—what good things I can make for others. Allow your image to shape my life, both in what I do and how I do it.

Making It Real

Have you recently created something that is really good, like a meal or a shed or a program? Did you know that you were reflecting God when you did that? This week, when it's time to make something, remember the One who made you and consider that you were created to create, just like Him. What one step will you take today to create, enrich or enhance something in your life?

For Further Exploration

For more consideration of how we were created to reflect God's image, read Anthony A. Hoekema's *Created in God's Image* (Grand Rapids, MI: William B. Eerdmans Publishing, 1994).

Will the Real Jesus Please Stand Up?

I believe in Jesus Christ . . .

And how about you? Who do you say I am? [26]
—JESUS

Few people would argue against the existence of Jesus Christ, given the historical evidence documenting His time on Earth. So why is He such a controversial figure, with volumes more written about Him than any other great leader in history?

The debate centers not on *whether* Jesus was but on *who* Jesus was—and who He is not. While nonreligious people and those of other faiths acknowledge Him to be a great man—a prophet even—the Bible identifies Him as something far more. He is God, both the Bible and Jesus Himself declared. A bold statement indeed. And one that ultimately cost His life.

So what? you may wonder. What difference does His life—divine or not—make today? Isn't it enough to simply admire and strive to follow His teachings?

Even if you do hold to the belief that Jesus is more than just a good man, what right do you have to claim that your view has more validity than anyone else's? Tragically, much of the discussion about the nature of Jesus seems to pivot around who's right and who's wrong rather than around the question of how belief in His divinity changes one's life.

Rather than simply angling for a lock on the truth, shouldn't we be examining the implications of embracing that truth? And shouldn't any truth worth fighting for hold implications beyond ourselves? Rather than providing an opportunity for one-upmanship, shouldn't that truth lead us to affect the world around us in ways that we could never pull off on our own, giving purpose and meaning to our lives and connecting us to something better than this broken world can offer?

For me, the search for Jesus' true identity originated out of my own sense of brokenness, not out of a desire to be right or to force my beliefs down anyone else's throat. Life, for me, lacked meaning and purpose. And this wasn't just a subtle underlying issue. To my way of thinking, simply lacking a good reason to exist was a good enough reason to die. The Danish philosopher Søren Kierkegaard once said that we tend to find a level of despair we can tolerate and call it normal.[27] I guess for me, the despair just never normalized.

That's why I relate so well to Peter, the fisherman who was ready and willing to drop his fishing nets and follow Jesus when he saw the prospect of something beyond the despair of "normal" life.

At one particularly low point when many were deserting Him, Jesus asked the remaining disciples, "Do you also want to leave?" Peter answered, "Master, to whom would we go? You have the words of real life, eternal life. We've already committed ourselves, confident that you are the Holy One of God."[28]

For Peter, believing in Jesus wasn't about having found the truth so that he could bang it over everyone else's head. Rather, the truth had found him, and he wasn't going to let it go, no matter what. Enduring the worst with Jesus was infinitely better than experiencing the best without Him.

I share Peter's perspective on faith. Sure, following Jesus is hard, and it has cost me a great deal. Believing is hard, and doubts often assail me. Reorienting my life around those beliefs is harder still, having to continually question my motives about who it is I'm trying to please.

But I've lived long enough without Him to know that existing without faith is a lot harder—without faith there is only emptiness, loneliness, hopelessness, lack of meaning and the utter despair of having to be my own god and figure it all out on my own. Who needs that kind of life—if you can call it a life at all?

What about you? Has the pain of living without Jesus surpassed the pain of giving up all to find Him? Those who first penned the Apostles' Creed lived in the reality that saying the words "I believe in Jesus Christ" could well cost them their lives. As a matter of fact, 10 of the original 12 apostles died as martyrs.

Closer to home, the cost of saying the words "I believe" is more likely to demand the laying down of selfish ambition. Releasing the illusion of control. Being ridiculed or unpopular. But in the words of the twentieth-century missionary martyr, Jim Elliot, "He is no fool who gives what he cannot keep to gain that which he cannot lose."[29]—SL

A Conversation with God

Dear Jesus, I want to know you. Not just about you, but to really know you. I commit myself to that task this month, and ask that you will meet me and reveal yourself to me in ways that right now I can't even fathom.

Making It Real

Imagine that you're introducing Jesus to a friend who has never met Him. Finish this opening line: "This is Jesus. I know you've never met Him before, but He's . . ." Fill in the blank with whatever you think is most important for your friend to know about Jesus.

Reflect for a minute on where you've gained your perception of who He is and what He is like. Are you satisfied with your insights on Him? If not, why?

For Further Exploration

An intriguing look at who Jesus really is, without all of the religious folklore, can be found in Philip Yancey's *The Jesus I Never Knew* (Grand Rapids, MI: Zondervan Publishing House, 2002).

Where Is God When I Feel Lonely?

I believe in Jesus Christ, **his only Son...**

The moment Jesus came up out of the baptismal waters, the skies opened up and he saw God's Spirit—it looked like a dove—descending and landing on him. And along with the Spirit, a voice: "This is my Son, chosen and marked by my love, delight of my life." [30]

—MATTHEW, DESCRIBING GOD (IN ALL THREE PERSONS) AT JESUS' BAPTISM

History recounts a time period called the Dark Ages—an era of barbarianism, fear and repression. I don't know about you, but that's pretty much how I'd describe my middle-school years. While the overall pressures of those formative years was often excruciating, if I had to summarize my experience with one word, it would be "lonely." Sure, I had friends and family, and I did okay in school. I even had fun participating in sports.

But I remember feeling lonely. A lot.

Looking back, I'd say it was my fear of being reject-ed or left out that prompted me to hold back, never feeling completely safe. I believed that if people really knew me, they'd want nothing to do with me. Or worse yet, they might even make fun of me.

For many of us, the "Dark Ages" didn't end with the passage of middle school. Loneliness has expanded into lifelong emptiness. And no matter how many people comprise our circle of friends and family, there remains a nagging void of authentic connections.

Though we may try to fill that void with any number of other things, the fact remains that we are relational beings. Humans are made in God's image, and He is Himself, even *within* Himself, a relational being. Christians have referred to this as the Trinity, a concept that describes the one true God as having always existed as three per-sons—Father, Son, and Holy Spirit—yet one essence.[31]

The story of Jesus' baptism beautifully illustrates how the Father, Son, and Spirit are related to one anoth-er. Looking again at the verse that opens this chapter, notice the kind of interaction they enjoyed: touching, talking, delighting, listening, choosing and loving. There is no fear or loneliness. This is intimacy and com-munity at its best.

This is just the kind of intimacy that we were created for, not only with each other but also with God Himself. When we are connected to God and people, we are living out our natural design to be like Him. I'm sure you have tasted this, in part, with a really good friend, your spouse or maybe one of your children. Like when you're just sitting together on the couch. At times there is not even a need for words. The moment is pregnant and full of the presence and enjoyment of one another.

So what keeps us from connecting like this more consistently? Why do most of us feel lonely, even among a group of friends?

While there may be many reasons, one primary obstacle that sticks out to me is fear. Just as my fear of rejection left me stuck in loneliness in middle school—and sometimes still does today—many of us hide from connecting in relationships with God and others. Sometimes we fear rejection, other times we fear commitment. Often, we fear both.

With God, we worry that He is angry with us or that He'll ask more from us than we can give. With people, we may think that if they *really* knew us, they'd choose more interesting or dynamic friends. Or, if we *really* knew them, they would demand too much from us.

The bad news is that whenever we allow our fears to keep us from truly connecting in relationships, we miss out on the kind of authentic relationships we were made for.

The good news is that it doesn't *have* to be this way. As a matter of fact, our relationships can be much deeper, more meaningful, and even enjoyable with *both* God and others. But we have some work to do.

First, nurturing healthy relationships requires us to keep facing our fears. It's normal to be afraid; we all are. But we must not allow our fears to keep us from enjoying what's beyond them, namely the deeper connections we desire with God and others.

Second, we must look for ways to get past the superficial levels in which most of our relationships get stuck. This involves taking more time with others, becoming more honest and real with them, holding back less.

It's risky, but the rewards are well worth the effort. Just imagine what it would be like to experience the community and intimacy shared by the Trinity—to live in the relationships for which you were created.—*CM*

A Conversation with God

Dear Father, Son, and Spirit, thank you for being the Being of Community. Thank you for generously allowing me the chance to live with others—in my family and in my friendships—as a reflection of you. Help me to think beyond superficial connections and to create real and meaningful relationships, like the ones you enjoy together.

Making It Real

How honest or real would you say your relationship with God is? How about with other people? List some obstacles you suspect might be keeping you from more authenticity in your relationships.

Take your list and use it to have a heart-to-heart conversation with God about where you are and where you'd like to be in your relationship with Him and with others.

For Further Exploration

A great book on this topic is Larry Crabb's *Connecting: Healing for Ourselves and Our Relationships* (Nashville, TN: Word Publishing, 1997).

What Does God Want from Me?

I believe in Jesus Christ, his only Son, **our Lord** . . .

Anyone who intends to come with me has to let me lead.[32]
—JESUS TO HIS FOLLOWERS

What is it about some people that drives others to imitate their clothes, their haircuts, their lifestyles? Perhaps more to the point, why do so many of us seem to be searching for someone to follow and pattern our lives after?

We might expect such behavior during the uncertainties of adolescence, with young women dressing (or undressing) like the latest MTV star, while young men mirror the styles of whoever happens to be "in" in their circles.

Yet maturity doesn't seem to spell an end to mimicry. Not long ago, Regis Philbin's wardrobe prompted a move toward monochromatic shirt-and-tie combos among businessmen, and "hairstyles of the stars" is a perennial hit feature for women's magazines. For years Nike found marketing success in encouraging consumers to "Be Like Mike," meaning, of course, Michael Jordan, who was so popular at the time that some said he was the single most recognizable face in the world— even more recognizable than the Pope. These days, reality TV shows are finding success by creating an obstacle course of challenges for individuals who want to be the apprentice to a successful celebrity or business mogul.

Apparently we feel a pull deep within to admire and emulate something outside ourselves. Welcome to the concept the church has traditionally called "discipleship." While the word often conjures up images of a highly structured behavioral program or of mastering some set of religious facts, the concept of discipleship is actually exhilarating when we understand what it means and how it drives our lives toward God.

Discipleship isn't simply some formula for spiritual growth or a set of rules for personal purity. Discipleship is about making decisions and purposefully emulating the best possible person we could imitate—Jesus Christ! It's about decisions made in light of the life, teachings, and even the death and resurrection of Jesus, which leads us into the life that God designed us for.

Listen to what Jesus said to that original group of followers:

Anyone who intends to come with me has to let me lead. You're not in the driver's seat; *I* am. Don't run from suffering; embrace it. Follow me and I'll show you how. Self-help is no help at all. Self-sacrifice is the way, my way, to saving yourself, your true self. What good would it do to get everything you want and lose you, the real you? What could you ever trade your soul for?[33]

Jesus has posed the fundamental question of discipleship: What would you trade your soul for? (What price will you pay tomorrow just to get your way today?) As you consider your answer, think about the word "discipleship," which literally means "to apprentice or attach yourself to someone."[34]

To what or to whom have you attached yourself? Or in the language of the Creed, who is your Lord? We all are apprentices of someone or something. We all have attached ourselves to some philosophy of life; generally it's all about us, what fits our vision of happiness or even our momentary moods.

Everyday decisions arise out of the driving force in our lives, which serves as a sort of mental checkpoint or filter. In a nanosecond we wonder, *Is this going to help me get what I want?* If the answer is yes, then it's likely that we will go ahead and do it. Sometimes the choice is deliberate: *I don't like the way she's treating me. I'm going to give her a piece of my mind!* Other choices are more subconscious, like hitting the snooze button when the alarm shrieks its obnoxious warning. *(Please, just nine more minutes!)*

But then Jesus' statement intrudes into our self-focused lives: "Anyone who intends to come with me has to let me lead." In other words, "Attach your decision-making to me." He wants center stage in our lives. To say that Jesus is our Lord or that we are His disciples is to say that we are learning to make decisions based on a question other than, Will this get me what I want? Instead, our choices are shaped by a Christ-centered question, Will this honor, reflect, follow, or emulate the life and teaching of Christ?

The amazing thing is that this kind of decision making—with Christ as our filter rather than simply our own interests—actually results in our deeper concerns and longings being quenched.

"Self-help is no help at all. Self-sacrifice is the way, my way, to saving yourself, your true self," says Jesus. Have you begun to discover this? That will depend on who or what you are attached to.—*CM*

A Conversation with God

Dear Jesus, sometimes I resist calling you Lord, afraid to let go of my self-reliance. Help me give up my

*demand to call the shots in my life and instead embrace
your leadership and guidance for me. Show me how to
make decisions that reflect your goodness and compassion rather than my own self-interests. Help me to live
as if you are not simply Lord, but my Lord.*

Making It Real

As you think about what it means to call Jesus "Lord,"
experiment this week with one difficult decision.
Rather than simply going with your intuition, advice
from friends or your own knee-jerk reaction, consider
what might best reflect the life and teaching of Jesus.
Then make your decision with Christ at the center,
rather than self.

For Further Exploration

An immensely popular book that addresses finding
purpose in one's life is Rick Warren's *The Purpose-
Driven Life* (Grand Rapids, MI: Zondervan Publishing
House, 2002).

Are Miracles for Real?

. . . who was conceived by the Holy Spirit . . .

Nothing, you see, is impossible with God.[35]
—THE ANGEL GABRIEL, REASSURING MARY

Have you ever witnessed a miracle? Many people, including me, thought they had seen just that during the Winter Olympics of 1980. As a 12-year-old, I was crazy about hockey. I knew that the Soviets—"the Russians," as we called them—had trounced Team USA in a pre-Olympic exhibition game. The previous year, the Soviets had crushed an NHL All-Star team. It seemed as if the Russians were invincible on ice and that the Americans were doomed to defeat.

Then it happened. We won. I can still hear Al Michaels, the sports commentator, screaming as the clock wound down, "Five seconds left in the game! Do you believe in miracles? Yes!"

I had goose bumps the size of Texas, and my eyes welled up with emotion. *Yes, I do!* I thought. Surely this was a miracle.

Or was it? It was an extraordinary turn of events, to be sure. It surpassed all of our hopes and dreams. But was it really a miracle? A miracle is defined as "an event or effect contrary to the established constitution and course of things, or a deviation from the known laws of nature; a supernatural event, or one transcending the ordinary laws by which the universe is governed."[36]

No doubt about it: that win was "contrary to the established course of things." By these standards, it was a miracle. But there were natural explanations for Team USA's victory over the Soviets that night. While watching *Miracle,* a movie about the 1980 Olympics, I thought, *Oh, so that's why it happened.* It was a bit of a let-down, like learning the secret behind a magic trick.

Imagine, for a minute, a different scene. What if Team USA had sprouted wings and flown around the rink to win that game, superseding nature itself? Talk about shocking the world! There would have been no natural explanation. That would have been a miracle by a different set of standards—supernatural ones.

The Apostles' Creed declares this is the kind of miracle that led to Mary becoming the mother of Jesus. Something beyond the laws of nature interfered in the established order of things. There is no explanation, at least none that we can understand. The Spirit formed one life within another, transcending the natural process of reproduction. God created a baby without using the typical raw materials. Now that's a *real* miracle.

I must admit that it's easier for me to believe in miracles that—while extraordinary or super-surprising—have some sort of natural explanation. For example, I know that even the biggest underdog can win an upset against incredible odds.

But *real* miracles—the kind that are totally inexplicable and *super*natural—are much harder for me to accept. My mind wants to reject anything it can't comprehend, so I search for explanations that might help me believe. Even Mary, after hearing God's intentions for her new baby asked, "But *how*?"

To our frustration, it often seems as if God doesn't share our interest in explanations. You'll note that Gabriel's response to Mary's question is a bit vague on the details, as is any answer that comes of our inquiries into miracles. But would getting an explanation really help? Granted, with increased clarity comes stronger reason to trust. But clarity isn't always possible. Maybe even if God explained Himself, I just wouldn't get it. Imagine a university professor trying to explain quantum physics to my eight-year-old son (or to me, for that matter). It's too much to take in.

What if it's like that with God and us? Even if He did explain to us the method behind a miracle, could we understand it? Probably not. But that's okay, isn't it? We don't insist on understanding electricity before we turn on a light. We don't wait for complete comprehension on how our car works before we hop into the driver's seat. We take these things on faith, trusting before we understand, knowing that we may never understand them at all. That's why we place our faith in experts, such as electricians and auto mechanics.

Why not give God the same benefit? In our relationship with Him, understanding isn't the primary issue; trust is. Nothing is impossible for Him. This gives us security and hope beyond our own limited comprehension. Not everything is dependent on our efforts. The pressure we often feel to make things happen can be relieved by faith in a God who can and does perform miracles.

The angel Gabriel said to Mary, "the child you bring to birth will be called Holy, the Son of God."[37] It's almost as if God is saying, "Trust me on this, Mary, even if you don't understand. . . ." I think He asks the same thing from each of us, for as the Bible says:

> Faith . . . is the firm foundation under everything that makes life worth living. It's our handle on what we can't see.[38]—CM

A Conversation with God

Dear Father, believing not only that you can do miracles but that you did this one in particular, through the Holy Spirit, changes things for me. My life isn't just in my hands, it's in yours. I don't have to do it all; I can trust in your power beyond my own.

I pray for you to bring your Spirit into my life, as you did with Mary. Help me to trust you and your reasons for things, ordinary or extraordinary, even when I may not fully understand.

Making It Real

What is the most insurmountable problem in your life right now? How might accepting God's power to perform miracles change your perspective about that issue?

For Further Exploration

For an engaging look at the possibility and probability of miracles from an intellectual standpoint, check out C. S. Lewis's *Miracles* (San Francisco: HarperSanFrancisco, 2001).

Does God Really Care About Our Puny Lives?

. . . and born of the Virgin Mary . . .

The Word became flesh and blood, and moved into the neighborhood.[39]

—JOHN, THE APOSTLE

When my brother stops by our house, everything in "kid-land" comes to a screeching halt. One of my offspring will spot his van (or hear his motorcycle) pulling up in the driveway and announce "Uncle Bryan's here!" like he's some kind of celebrity. Before my brother can even take off his jacket, they'll be asking all sorts of questions about what he's doing, how long he's staying, or whether he'll wrestle with them or play Nintendo. None of it fazes him. Before long, he's down on the floor with a joystick in his hand or a giggling kid in his arms.

What is it about Bryan that so captivates my kids? I'd say it's the fact that he hasn't lost touch with their world. He remembers what it's like to be too short to see what's on top of the refrigerator or to be snubbed by being sent to the kid's table during large family gatherings. Unlike most of us boring grownups, he doesn't worry about getting dirty on the floor. My kids love Uncle Bryan because, in their eyes, he's one of them. He lives in their neighborhood. He speaks their language. He loves them—and he just plain likes kids.

Like Bryan, God knows what it takes to truly connect with someone's way of life. Unlike other gods who watch their subjects from afar or remain just out of reach, He has become one of us. He gets dirty, down on the floor, wrapping His arms around us. He loves us. And He just plain likes us.

He knows what it's like to be too short to see things in heaven. He's lived with the snub of being left out. This, *the Incarnation*, is what is celebrated at Christmas—that God took on flesh, was born into our world, and—as the apostle John phrased it—moved into our neighborhood.

While He could have accomplished His purposes in some other way, God chose to allow His Son to endure the reality of life on Earth. The apostle Paul wrote:

When the time came, [Jesus] set aside the privileges of deity and took on the status of a
slave, became *human!* . . . It was an incredibly humbling process. He didn't claim special
privileges. Instead, he lived a selfless, obedient
life and then died a selfless, obedient death—
and the worst kind of death at that: a crucifixion.[40]

Somehow, God understood our need to connect
with someone who could relate to our pain and disappointment. What is it that feels so comforting about
finding another person who has experienced whatever
it is you're facing? Why is connecting with someone
like this so powerful? One particular event in my life
points to the power of such a connection.

A few months into our marriage, my wife and I
made the joyful discovery that she was pregnant. We
eagerly awaited the opportunity to welcome this new
little life into our home and began making all sorts of
plans for the house and our lives.

But everything came to a screeching halt the afternoon she began showing signs that the little one in her
womb was in danger. The doctors sent us home,
telling us that all we could do was wait. Eventually, we
found ourselves in the emergency room facing the

grim confirmation that our child was gone. We had lost our first baby.

Our grief was penetratingly deep, even though we had never even seen (except through an ultrasound) or met our child. Friends and family embraced us with cards, phone calls, flowers and tears. Yet despite all their gestures of comfort, we felt utterly alone.

As we drifted on this ocean of pain, our spirits were buoyed a bit whenever we encountered a certain kind of person. It wasn't a therapist or a pastor or a medical expert, although some things offered by each of these people did help. The most powerful support came from those who had lost a child themselves.

These people had survived a similar grief, and as a result could offer a beyond-natural kind of comfort. They remembered. They felt our loss as their own. Having navigated this route before us, they were equipped to speak the words we needed to hear—and to know when the time called for silence. Their connection to us didn't make us less sad, but it somehow made us feel less alone. They were with us. They knew us.

As you get to know God, you begin to realize He *knows* you. When Jesus was misunderstood by His own family and the religious community and was even betrayed by His best friends, He knew excruciating relational pain. When His friend Lazarus died, He wept in grief, experiencing emotional pain. When He was beaten and crucified on the cross, he experienced intense physical pain. The spiritual torment He must have felt when He cried out to His Father, "Why have you forsaken me?" is beyond words. Jesus has experienced every facet of human pain that we will ever face.

We all want to connect with someone who understands the depth of our experience. God Himself can connect with us in just that way. He lowered Himself to the floor to wrestle with life here on Earth. He has lived our reality. He speaks our language.

Who wouldn't want to spend time with a God like that?—*CM*

A Conversation with God

Dear Father, do you really know our world—my world? Sometimes it feels like you don't know what it's like down here. I wonder if you see what I see and hear what I hear. Help me to trust, even if I don't understand, that you know what I know; that you know even more than I know. Help me to see today that you are still with me, with all of us. Thank you for coming down and getting dirty for me.

Making It Real

Is there something in your life that is particularly difficult and you wonder if God really understands? Write Him a letter, a prayer, explaining what you are going through in as much detail as you need. Then explain, as best you can, what you imagine Jesus must have gone through to be born into this world. End the letter by asking God to speak into your life in your language—through friends, prayer, Scripture—and seal it with a promise to listen for Him.

For Further Exploration

For a wonderfully refreshing look at how much God loves us—and likes us—read Brennan Manning's *The Ragamuffin Gospel: Embracing the Unconditional Love of God* (Sisters, OR: Multnomah, 1990).

How Can God Understand What I'm Going Through?

He suffered under Pontius Pilate . . .

Since he himself has now been through suffering and temptation, he knows what it is like when we suffer and are tempted, and he is wonderfully able to help us. . . . He understands our weaknesses, since he had the same temptations we do, though he never once gave way to them and sinned.[41]

—THE AUTHOR OF HEBREWS, REFERRING TO JESUS

I had heard so much about Annette. And now I would have the chance to meet her.

She and her husband were missionaries in western Europe when she began to have pain in her back. When the pain became so unbearable that she could no longer function, even with muscle relaxants, X-rays revealed a tumor the size of a grapefruit, which had attached itself to her spinal cord. Though surgery would need to be done immediately, the operation was considered somewhat routine and not a particularly high-risk procedure.

Something went wrong, however. Annette awakened from the surgery paralyzed from the neck down and in constant, excruciating pain. Not long afterward, she, her husband and their five children returned to the United States where she could be cared for in more appropriate surroundings.

Now, years after this tragedy changed her life, Annette's husband had invited me to their home for Sunday dinner. I had always admired her, having heard how she refused pain-numbing medications so that she wouldn't also be numbed to all of life. Yet I wasn't sure what to expect from my visit. Would she be bed-bound? Would we only be able to communicate a few minutes before she needed rest?

What I encountered when I entered their home was a beautifully dressed woman whose outward expression revealed little of her physical pain. During my five-hour visit, Annette served as a gracious hostess who shared her story with honesty.

She told how when she first came out of the surgery, she and everyone else focused on praying for God to heal her. When that didn't happen and she was confined to 24-hour care at home, she became very depressed. Most people stopped connecting with her.

Their lives moved on while Annette's came to a screeching halt. Bible college and missionary training had not equipped her to deal with a life tied to a wheelchair and filled with constant pain.

"I felt that I was left with three choices," said Annette. "To kill myself and end the unbearable suffering for all of us; to abandon my faith in God and merely exist on painkillers; or to put my energies to discovering God in the midst of all of this suffering.

Annette's face beamed. "I chose the third," she said. "And as I began slowly reading the Bible again through the lens of pain and suffering, what I saw was a God who was familiar with both. I thought my pain and suffering had taken me to a place where God could never be found; instead, it was a place where He became more real to me than I had ever known Him to be."

What an incredible outlook! That conversation with Annette transformed my view of pain. While I certainly would never choose suffering—who in their right mind would?—I've also come to realize that I can't escape it. It's part of living in a fallen world. But as Annette so poignantly explains, pain is a gift from God, a means of connecting with Him in new and unprecedented ways.

God's personal experience in suffering is most clearly revealed in the life of Jesus. I had always spouted that the reason for the crucifixion was so that the penalty for sin could be paid. I still believe this, but the full truth seems to extend well beyond just that. God could have accomplished a painless death and resurrection for His Son up in heaven in a millisecond. Why send Him to Earth to suffer all that He did while living here for 33 years?

I believe He chose that route to offer comfort to people like Annette who live in constant pain and suffering. To offer comfort to people like me and you who experience pain on a regular basis and wonder, *Where is God in all of this?*

The Bible says that Jesus suffered and was tempted in every way that we are so that He could know firsthand what we are going through and walk with us in it.

I've actually found this truth to be of great help in the midst of my darkest moments when I find myself wondering, *Where has God experienced this?* Where has He experienced the pain of parenting a wayward child; the suffering of feeling misunderstood and wrongly accused; the horror of betrayal; physical pain and torment; the temptation that seems beyond my ability to withstand; the sadness, grief and depression that bring me to despair? Inevitably, I find within the Bible an occasion on which God Himself walked through something similar. And mysteriously, He does so again as He accompanies me right into the depth of my own experience.

Annette described it as the "fellowship of sharing in His sufferings."[42]

As I prepared to leave that day, she told me, "I'm not saying I would wish my experience on anyone, but it is the path God has chosen for me. And I wouldn't trade it for anything."

Can you say the same?—*SL*

A Conversation with God

God, it's amazing that you would choose to suffer—and that part of the reason is so that you can relate to me and walk with me in the suffering and pain of my life. Help me to connect with and find you in that place today.

Making It Real

Consider what you know of the life of Christ. Which of His experiences in some way parallel your own pain, suffering or frustration?

How did Christ handle those situations?

In what ways might your connection with Christ help you in what you're going through?

For Further Exploration

For a frank and honest exploration of feeling frustrated with God, read Philip Yancey's *Disappointment with God: Three Questions No One Asks Aloud* (Grand Rapids, MI: Zondervan Publishing House, 1988).

Do We Have to Bring Up Dying?

He . . . **was crucified, died,** and was buried . . .

By embracing death, taking it into himself, he destroyed the Devil's hold on death and freed all who cower through life, scared to death of death.[43]

—THE WRITER OF HEBREWS REFERRING TO JESUS

I had just finished having lunch with a friend and was on my way back to my office when what began as a twinge of indigestion suddenly turned into something much more severe. The pains in my chest became excruciating and then my left arm began to throb as well.

I didn't dare say the words out loud, but fear flooded my mind: *I'm having a heart attack!*

Having left my cell phone at the office, I couldn't dial 9-1-1. Initially, I hoped to drive to the hospital, but I soon had to pull off to the side of the road for fear that I might pass out.

As I sat in my car, I prayed, "God, please don't let me die. I'm not ready to die. My kids need a dad. Hanne isn't able to take on everything as a single mom and to be without me.

"If You spare my life, I promise I'll be a better dad and a more loving husband. I'll serve You more whole-heartedly." And on I went, recounting every area of my life that was of utmost importance to me, yet had somehow been pushed from center stage, crowded out by my chronic busyness and multiple commitments.

As you've probably guessed by now, I didn't die that afternoon. In fact, I didn't even have a heart attack. As near as I can tell, it was the Italian food. But the experience shook me up enough that I took part of the next day off and spent a significant amount of time praying and thinking about life—and about death. And re-prioritizing how I was living.

Funny how the prospect of dying can do that, huh? Perhaps you've had a similar experience, when the things that used to seem so complicated suddenly become very simple. A child's illness, the death of a friend, a cancer scare—nothing like a look at death to remind us that life is a gift. And a fragile one at that.

Death can be such a robber of life, not just because the end often comes abruptly and without warning but, even more so, because our fear of dying often keeps us from really living. We tend to cower through life, as the Scripture puts it, trying to deny the inevitable by hoarding, self-protecting or shutting down and simply existing rather than truly living. I believe it was Benjamin Franklin who said, "Most men die at age 25, we just don't bury them until 65."

Such an attitude is in direct opposition to how Jesus lived. Even though His death was ever before Him, He didn't allow it to suck the life out of Him. In fact, His awareness of it seemed to motivate Him to live all the more fully, to give Himself without reservation.

Maybe part of the reason He could embrace life so fully was because He also embraced death. He knew that death wasn't the true enemy, and that it wouldn't have the last word. Yes, this life would end—in His case, by a brutal crucifixion—but He was also aware that what awaited Him on the other side would be utterly glorious and well worth the cost.

Similarly, I've found that in coming to grips with death, I can actually embrace life more fully, knowing that God holds my future and that death is not the ultimate end but an opening into a whole new dimension.

Dietrich Bonhoeffer, the famous Lutheran theologian who was imprisoned in a Nazi concentration camp in 1944, powerfully exhibited his belief in that reality. The knowledge that death lurked at his doorstep could not snuff life from him. In fact, it did quite the opposite. In the last letter Bonhoeffer wrote to his best friend before his execution, he said:

> I am still discovering right up to this very moment that it is only in living completely in this world that we experience true life and faith. By this I mean living unreservedly in life's duties, problems, successes and failures. In so doing we throw ourselves completely into the arms of God. Taking seriously not only our problems, but those of God and the world. That, I think, is faith.[44]

Bonhoeffer's writings from that Nazi camp continue to impact countless lives today, bearing testimony to the words of Scripture: "Where, O death, is your victory? Where, O death, is your sting?"[45] —SL

A Conversation with God

Dear God. I thank you that my present and my future are secure in you. Help me to orient my life so that I can risk living and loving fully, just as Jesus did. Show me the opportunities before me today to choose life, and make me aware of those times when I don't.

Making It Real

If you knew that you only had six months to live, how would you prioritize your life differently?

What would it take to reorder your life according to those priorities today? Write down your thoughts, and then choose to make at least one change this week.

For Further Exploration

One of the best books on living life to the fullest is a little volume by Anthony DeMello, *The Way to Love*, (New York: Doubleday, 1995).

Day 15

Who Said Words Could Never Hurt You?

He . . . was crucified, died, **and was buried.**

God made him who had no sin to be sin for us, so that in him we might become the righteousness of God.[46]

—THE APOSTLE PAUL

When I was growing up, pants for boys came in three styles: slim, regular and husky.

You can probably guess which style I wore (or why would I have even bothered to bring it up?).

Even though the label wasn't posted on the outside of the pants (unlike some manufacturers that publish the waist and inseam sizes for all to see), I still begged my mother to buy me slims, or even regulars, and cut six inches off the bottom of the legs. She wouldn't. To this day I feel the indignity of being labeled a "husky."

I'm sure the "slims" have never given their label a second thought.

Sad to say, I've picked up a lot of other labels through the years. Some were given to me by others; several I've slapped on myself. And most of these monikers have been far more destructive than the ones on my pants as a youth.

Like political attack ads, labels are an attempt to categorize complex and multifaceted individuals under simple and concise headings such as liar, cheater, codependent, alcoholic, failure, weakling, Attention Deficit Disordered, adulterer, abused, insecure, untrustworthy.

Such labels tend to stick with us long after others have forgotten tagging them on us. Like a high-school girl I know named Jenny, who weighs less than 80 pounds when she should weigh 126. When I talked to Jenny about the anorexic label that doctors have posted on her chart, she revealed that her diagnosis is not the label she owns—or the one that owns her. The label she claims as her own came from a junior-high kid who blurted out "fatso" and made *oink* sounds in front of the entire cafeteria when she was picking up her lunch tray some four years ago. It's unlikely that he even remembers that day, and it's just as unlikely that she'll ever forget.

So how do we rid ourselves of such destructive labels? How do we erase the messages that loop through our thoughts, chanting, *You'll never amount to anything. You're just like your mother. No one could ever love you. If people knew the* real *you, you wouldn't have a friend in the world.*

Yes, we need to own what we've done and accept the truth that we can improve in certain areas. But we don't need to wear failure as a permanent badge, as if our worst action or weakest trait somehow depicts the sum total of who we are.

Because labels can attach themselves so deeply to our inner being, liberating ourselves requires a deliberate process of dying to each and burying them, never again to resurrect them. Of course, that's much easier said than done. I know from working with inmates that a person can be freed from prison in an instant, but the process of shedding the prisoner mind-set can take years, or even a lifetime. Maybe that's part of the reason for the radical nature of the Cross and the Crucifixion.

God's work with us is not confined to incremental personal growth or self-improvement. He is about transformational change—change that begins with an altered identity that's not bound to past actions and labels but is rooted in the identity of Jesus Christ. The Bible says, "If anyone is in Christ, he is a new creation; the old has gone, the new has come!"[47]

So, how does that happen? It all starts with Jesus. According to the Bible passage at the start of this reading, Jesus was the perfect man. Though not everyone followed Him, as far as labels resulting from evil or sinful actions go, He had none.

Yet on the Cross, all of our destructive and sinful labels were put upon Him. He bore the weight of the sins of the world. In that moment, He became the most sin-filled man on the face of the Earth—not because of His actions but because of what was transferred onto Him. The biblical word for this is "impute," an accounting term that means: "to reckon over unto another's account."[48]

Jesus took upon Himself all of our sin and all of the labels that identify us with that destructive nature. And then He died with them, on the cross. He carried them to hell. The price was paid for them, and according to God, they're gone.

And then, when death was conquered at the Resurrection, a whole new set of labels was imputed to us: accepted, forgiven, eternally secured, cherished, son or daughter of God, entrusted with purpose.

We are new people, and those labels call us to a whole new way of being!—SL

A Conversation with God

Dear God, right now I choose to believe what you have said about me, over what others—and even I—

*have decided is true. Thank you that you have
already made up your mind about how you feel
about me. I don't need to do another thing to be
loved and accepted by you. I just receive it. Help me
to then "live up to what [I] have already attained"
(Philippians 3:15).*

Making It Real

Make two columns here or on another sheet of paper. Label the first column: *Destructive labels that have been attached to me.* Over the second column write: *Labels that God has given to me.* Under each heading, fill in as many words or phrases as you can. Then scratch out the labels on the left one at a time, and at the same time detach yourself from that identity. Now circle each one on the right as a deliberate act of owning what God has said to be true about you.

For Further Exploration

For intriguing insights on how God sees us as His children, read Brennan Manning's *Abba's Child: The Cry of the Heart for Intimate Belonging* (Colorado Springs, CO: NavPress, 1994).

Can Hell Be Much Worse than This?

If I make my bed in the depths, you are there. . . .
If I say, "Surely the darkness will hide me
and the light become night around me,"
even the darkness will not be dark to you. [49]

—KING DAVID, SPEAKING TO GOD

Have you ever taken the walking tour into Mammoth Cave in south central Kentucky? If not, picture this: The park ranger leads the group on a gradual descent deep inside the cave, and then turns off the flashlight. You can't even see your own hand held five inches in front of your face, let alone make out the silhouette of the person next to you. The darkness is overwhelming. And then fear starts to set in. Darkness has a way of making you feel isolated, immobilized, alone, lost, helpless.

After a few panic-stricken moments that seem much longer than they actually are, the guide strikes a match. Astoundingly, the entire canyon becomes illuminated. Peace overtakes fear.

According to the Apostles' Creed and to Scripture, Jesus, the Light of the world, descended all the way into the darkest pit in all of creation: hell—the place of the dead. It's a place He's quite familiar with, not just because of a brief visit there some 2,000 years ago, but because He regularly steps in to our personal hells to rescue us when we cry out to Him.

Can there be such a thing as "hell on earth"? The answer seems to be yes, if we consider hell a place of death. Each of us at different times will face a living death—the death of a dream, the death of a relationship, the death of meaning. I certainly have experienced that kind of hell many times, feeling utterly helpless in the face of tragedy and pain. As I've found myself alone in a dark and desolate place of depression, I've concluded that surely any physical hell couldn't be much worse than the torture I was enduring. But it's been in the midst of that hell on Earth that I've encountered God, as His light and love drive away the shadows in response to my desperate pleas.

Someone once said, "Religion is for those who don't want to go to hell. Spirituality is for those who've been there." I know what that person means. And yet, while this world does contain a good deal of hell, it also contains a lot of heaven, for God's hand is active throughout. I believe our earthly experiences of hell are merely a preview to the horrors of a hell that exists as a place outside Earth. The Bible speaks of it often.

I don't see this physical hell as a place handcrafted by a vengeful God to punish people who don't toe the line or succumb to His rule, as many have purported. Rather, I see hell as that place where the absence of God rules. Consequently, it's a place overrun with unbridled evil, pain, torture and misery. It is depression with no light at the end of the tunnel, no possibility of relief. For without God, there is no light, no love and no mercy to press against the darkness and the overwhelming sense of desolation.

Many people wrestle with the idea that a loving God would send anyone to such a place of torment, yet hell is a reality because God honors a person's decision to choose Him as well as a decision to reject Him. Hell is the ultimate fulfillment of a choice to live without God, forever. And that's what makes it hell.

It is certainly God's desire that no person experience hell, either on this earth or in the hereafter.[50] That's why Jesus went to the cross to serve the sentence for our sin, because we could never attain perfection on our own. It's why He descended to hell and continues to enter into our hellish pain today with His comfort and grace.

That's the good news. But that good news is transformed into overwhelming gratitude and delight when we consider the darkness and the despair from which we have been rescued.—SL

A Conversation with God

Dear God, thank you that there is no place I can go on this earth where you cannot reach me. Thank you for shining your light even into my darkest hell and for rescuing me from that place of despair. Please make me a beacon of your light, shining into the darkness around me so that others might see you as well.

Making It Real

Write down some of the ways you have experienced God entering your pain (through His own presence or through using other people) to drive back the darkness of hell.

Express your gratitude to God for where He has brought you. Find some expression that uniquely reflects your feelings—perhaps in the form of a song, poem, prayer, dance or a shout of praise.

For Further Exploration

For a unique perspective on encountering God in the midst of pain, consider Larry Crabb's *Shattered Dreams: God's Unexpected Path to Joy* (Colorado Springs, CO: WaterBrook Press, 2001).

Is There Life After Death?

The third day **he rose again from the dead . . .**

You're blessed when you're at the end of your rope.
With less of you there is more of God and his rule.[51]

—JESUS

It's a dreadful feeling to find yourself at the end of your rope, running out of resources, solutions and hope. You sense yourself free-falling into impending doom, totally out of control. Or worse yet, you feel as if someone else is ultimately in control of your destiny.

Jesus must have experienced such feelings as He entrusted Himself into the hands of evil people bent on snuffing Him out. I guess that's why He agonized so, on that night before His arrest and crucifixion, saying, "Father, if you are willing, take this cup from me; yet not my will, but yours be done."[52]

Maybe His response in the face of certain tragedy holds the secret to stepping into and surviving hell on

Earth: You can rest in the knowledge that, ultimately, you're not at the mercy of the clutches of people; rather, you're held securely in the arms of God.

Not only that, it's been my experience that when I allow God to walk with me into those flames that feel so deathlike, what He resurrects out of the ashes is actually something new and quite different from that which previously existed.

When I was 25, I experienced a sort of early mid-life crisis. (I say "early" because I've had several since then.) I was working as a stockbroker when I realized that all of my dreams had already come true. I guess that says less about my accomplishments and more about the shallowness of my dreams. Basically, I had just wanted to make a lot of money—and I had succeeded.

In a strange sort of way, I was at the end of my rope. If this was all there was to life—having a good job and plenty of money—I wasn't sure it was enough for me.

As part of that search for meaning and purpose, I traveled to China on a Bible-smuggling trip with four other people. During my time there, I heard about a pastor who had just been released from prison, where he had endured horrendous torture. It wasn't his first time behind bars, but with this release came a stern threat: "If we ever hear of you teaching the Bible in the unregistered church again, you will be executed."

When we met at an early morning prayer gathering of underground Christians, I was anxious to find out from him what it was like to suffer torture in a Chinese prison.

He simply smiled and said, "God has been very good to me."

When I returned home, I couldn't forget the life that I had seen in his eyes and that I had witnessed in the Chinese Christians I had met. Truthfully, I had a hard time going to work the first two or three days after I got back. I cried a lot. I looked around at all the things I had amassed—a sports car, a beautiful home, a very secure life. But it felt lifeless to me.

I knew nothing of the power, love and relationship with God that I had witnessed in my newfound Chinese friends. I'm sure that I had more Bible knowledge and many more tools to live out my faith, but they had experienced a resurrection power—a power that seemingly comes only on the other side of dying to self. I knew I wanted more of that for myself.

Is this power available only to a few "super saints" like that Chinese pastor? Not according to the apostle Paul, who said, "I pray that you will begin to understand how incredibly great his power is to help those who believe him. It is that same mighty power that raised Christ from the dead."[53] The Greek word for power is *dunamis,* from which comes the term "dynamite." Through the death and release of our own puny desires comes an explosive release of God's awesome power.

It's like Jesus said:

> Unless a grain of wheat is buried in the ground, dead to the world, it is never any more than a grain of wheat. But if it is buried, it sprouts and reproduces itself many times over. In the same way, anyone who holds on to life just as it is destroys that life. But if you let it go, reckless in your love, you'll have it forever, real and eternal.[54]

While I have never undergone persecution that even remotely resembles the experience of my Chinese brothers and sisters, each day offers countless opportunities to die to myself—to my pride, my selfishness, my own self-interests. And when I choose to surrender to Jesus, resting in the arms of God rather than striving to control my own destiny, I experience something of that same supernatural dynamite power that I could never generate on my own. It's the kind of life that seems to come only through death.—*SL*

A Conversation with God

God, I'm really hungry for more of you in my life.
I'm tired of living just for myself and missing a
dimension of your power that comes only when I lay
aside my own interests. Show me today where I can
choose you, where I can experience the power of
your resurrection life in me.

Making It Real

In what areas of your life do you sense God asking you
to die to self?

How might your life change if you choose to allow
Him to bring new life to that area?

For Further Exploration

A great book on finding greater purpose and meaning
in life is Max Lucado's *It's Not About Me: Rescue from the
Life We Thought Would Make Us Happy* (Brentwood, TN:
Integrity Publishers, 2004).

Is Heaven As Boring As It Sounds?

He ascended to heaven . . .

Then the Master Jesus, after briefing them, was taken up to heaven, and he sat down beside God in the place of honor. [55]

—FROM MARK'S GOSPEL

It's the moment every Sunday School teacher dreads: A waist-high, sniffling little rascal who knows just enough to be dangerous stumps you in front of a roomful of his mini-theologian friends.

A few years ago, I was cruising smoothly through a lesson about Jesus' final days on Earth. As we were discussing the Bible's description of Jesus going to be with His Father in heaven, up went the little hand of a boy named Johnny, and out shot the challenge: "Did

Jesus go up there to *do* something, or just to sit there with the Father?"

I got the sense that Johnny suspected, after all Jesus' hard work on Earth, that we might catch Him golfing in His heavenly retirement home (possibly with Johnny's grandparents?).

"Hmmm. Good question, Johnny," I said. "Maybe you should ask your mom and dad." (That's Sunday School code for "I don't know.") Johnny didn't flinch.

"And another thing, Mr. Chris. How could He be in heaven, with God, if He is here on Earth with us?"

Sometimes the curiosity of a child reinforces for me just how difficult Christian faith can be. I stumbled and mumbled my way through a vague response, but after class I continued thinking about what it means to *actually* believe this particular part of the creed: "he ascended to heaven . . ." If that's true, what is He doing there? And isn't He still *here* too, somehow?

After spending a little time on research, I wrestled my way to some basic conclusions. First, we can easily get stuck here, intellectually, unless we push our skeptical minds past a preference for either/or thinking. For whatever reason, many of us get caught in the trap of dichotomies. We believe the answer must be one or the other. Either we go left *or* we go right. Either Jesus is in heaven *or* He is on Earth. Pick one, but only one.

If we stop to think this through, we realize that not all choices are mutually exclusive. Is Boston in Massachusetts or in New England? Both, actually. When it comes to the nature of Christ, it's not as if Jesus has to be either in heaven or on Earth. If He really is God, not limited to time or space, He can be in both places at once—or even in all places at once. This is why we skeptics tend to get so tangled. We keep trying to find answers that make sense to our finite minds, forgetting that we're dealing with an infinite mystery.

If we can manage to set aside either/or thinking, we suddenly have room in our minds to consider that Jesus isn't just sitting around "up there." Near the end of His time on Earth, Jesus told His disciples that He was on His way to get their rooms ready. Then He promised, "I'll come back and get you so you can live where I live."[56] He's still working *for* us. He is preparing our rooms—our homes—in heaven. The great architect, designer and builder is working diligently to get everything just right for you and me.

Realizing that Jesus is *still* working, preparing heaven for us, reminds me how radically committed God is to our complete and total well-being here on Earth, just as He is in heaven. That's one of the reasons He sent the Holy Spirit, to help us (on Earth) get ready for Him (in heaven). We prepare for Him as He prepares for us.

This sounds easier than it is. Our hearts and minds are so full of distracting and temporary things that we need divine help to shift our focus to Him. As the apostle Paul urges, "Don't shuffle along, eyes to the ground, absorbed with the things right in front of you. Look up, and be alert to what is going on around Christ—that's where the action is."[57]

So as you're thinking about your future home and what it might be like, take a moment to consider this: If Jesus isn't sitting around waiting for eternity to begin, how should we be spending our time?—CM

A Conversation with God

Dear Father, I do get stuck in my limited ability to see things, to understand them. It's hard for me to grasp that Jesus could be both divine and human, both here on Earth and in heaven. Does it really matter? He said He is preparing a room for me. I'm not sure what that means, but I pray for your Spirit to be preparing me too. Help me to let go and to trust that you are working for me, and that I can work with you.

Making It Real

Today, pay special attention to those times that you limit possibilities with either/or thinking. Then use what you discover to examine how either/or thinking shapes your view of faith. For example, how do you view the "problem" of unanswered prayers? Is it that God *can't* do anything about your request or that He *won't*? Or is there another possibility? What if He's neither weak nor cruel but instead operates from reasons we cannot possibly understand?

For Further Exploration

A classic book on the mysteries of Christ and all aspects of Christian faith is C. S. Lewis's *Mere Christianity* (San Francisco: HarperSanFrancisco, 2001).

What Can I Depend On from God?

. . . and **is seated at the right hand of God** the Father almighty.

And who would dare tangle with God by messing with one of God's chosen? Who would dare even to point a finger? The One who died for us—who was raised to life for us!—is in the presence of God at this very moment sticking up for us.[58]

—THE APOSTLE PAUL

In his book *Love Beyond Reason*, pastor John Ortberg tells of sitting in the empty auditorium of the church building when one of his children said, "Daddy, preach to us." Seeing an opportunity to teach his three children about how God cares for them, Ortberg recounted to them a scene from the movie *The Bear*. In the film, a little cub loses his mother but is "adopted" by another huge Kodiak bear who protects him.

At one point, separated from his protector, the cub comes face to face with a mountain lion poised to pounce. John described the cub's response to his children: "He rears up on his hind legs, lifts his paws, and tries to growl fiercely, but the best he can manage is a squeak. The mountain lion is not convinced. Both the cub and his attacker know he is about to die."

Then all of a sudden, the lion turns around and bolts. You wonder what happened, until eventually you see what the lion saw. Behind the cub, the Kodiak stands his ground. The father reminds his children, "The cub couldn't see him or hear him, but the father was there all the time. . . . The father could be trusted, even when he seemed to be absent."[59]

Like that little cub, we all hope for and expect our parents to protect us when we are young. And when we become parents, we find ourselves gripped with the conviction that we'll risk nearly anything for our son or daughter.

This sort of passionate protection is what the Creed implies when it says that Jesus is sitting at the right hand of God. Far from simply noting His physical position, the phrase "sitting at the right hand of God" indicates that He is in a place of power, protecting us. Even if we can't see or hear Him, He stands His ground behind us, up on His hind legs, growling. As the apostle Paul wrote, Jesus "is in the presence of God at this very moment sticking up for us."[60]

So why is it that so few of us *feel* safe? We fear our vulnerability to financial pressure, the betrayal of loved ones, terrorism and all the unknowns that lurk in our future. When we're in the midst of crisis and pain, it certainly seems that we aren't very safe—at least not as safe as we'd like to be. Jesus may be sitting in the place of power and protection at the Father's right hand, but it appears that many of the "mountain lions" in life are unfazed by His growl.

So just how safe are we? If we interpret the Creed as claiming that all Christians are guaranteed some kind of spiritual Kevlar suit, then history gives us reason to fear that suit is flawed. But what if Jesus isn't necessarily working toward our *immediate* safety but instead is ad-dressing something far more important—our *ultimate* safety? Can we trust that while the big bear won't keep every thorn from poking into our paw, He will make sure that, in the end, nothing will pry us away from Him?

This is an enormously important distinction for people who want to trust God. It's one thing for a father to promise to stay with his son, no matter what, never letting anyone take him. It's another thing completely for that father to say that nothing will *try* to snatch the child away. God has not promised to insulate us from all pain and suffering. He promises that none of it can or will separate us from Him.

When this reality settles into our faith, it can be a bit of a letdown. Something in our controlling nature wants to believe that if we do our part (some form of being as good as we can be), then God is on the hook to do His part (protect us and our loved ones from pain). But that's not how this relationship works. God offers Himself to us regardless of whether or not we're being as good as we can be. He pursues us out of His grace, as a gift of His love, rather than as a response to our goodness.

As the reality of our Protector's true role settles in a bit further, disappointment can give way to hope. If it's true, as the Bible says, that our greatest enemies are sin and death,[61] then the growl of Jesus has in fact done its job. Sin no longer separates us from God, because of the life, death and resurrection of Jesus. Death has also lost its sting and is ultimately trampled by the Resurrection.

Listen to how Paul applies this concept in his life, as he explains to his friends in Rome: "I'm absolutely convinced that nothing—nothing living or dead, angelic or demonic, today or tomorrow, high or low, thinkable or unthinkable—absolutely nothing can get between us and God's love because of the way that Jesus our Master has embraced us."[62]

This is an invitation to live our lives with the security of knowing that we are never alone or unsafe. With that trust comes peace. Isn't *that* something we'd all like more of?—*CM*

A Conversation with God

Dear Father, I do wish that life had less pain and more joy. Sometimes I want to blame you for this. Sometimes I blame myself or even other people. Help me to actively trust in your promise that Jesus can and will protect me, that He is up on His hind legs, standing behind me, turning away anything that could or would ever take me from you. I want to see this in my mind's eye. I want to trust this. I want to help others see it too.

Making It Real

Physical, emotional and relational threats all have tremendous impact on how we see God, how much we trust Him and how we live out that trust. Think about the kinds of pain you've recently endured or the fears you might be facing, and then write out some of these things on a piece of paper. On the bottom of the paper, if you can authentically say this, write and offer the following prayer: "Father, with Jesus at your right hand protecting me, help me to trust that not even these things can take me away from you." Carry that prayer with you, in your wallet or purse, using it as a reminder of His protection over you and your trust in Him.

For Further Exploration

For fresh insights on seeing God in the midst of all that is happening in and around us, read Richard Rohr's *Everything Belongs: The Gift of Contemplative Prayer* (New York: Crossroads, 2003).

Who Wants to Be Judged?

From there **he will come to judge** the
living and the dead . . .

*And this is the judgment, that the light has come into
the world, and people loved darkness rather than light
because their deeds were evil.*[63]

—THE APOSTLE JOHN

What comes to mind when you read this portion of
the Apostles' Creed? God sitting up in heaven, finally
getting even with those who have refused to submit to
His impossible demands? Nervousness about whether
you've done enough good in your life to outweigh the
bad? The humiliation of having all your shameful acts
exposed and paraded before the world?

Certainly, the thought of being judged in this man-
ner is not pleasant to any of us. We all tend to run and
hide from the light when we believe its sole purpose is
to expose and punish that which is hidden.

But what if, rather than condemning us, exposure to God's light serves as our friend, allowing Him fuller access into our lives? What if His light is actually the path to healing, calling us out of the darkness of fear, shame, humiliation and death? God's desire is not to condemn us but to save us, says John 3:17. But He cannot help or heal that which is hidden or denied.

Who would visit a doctor and spend the entire appointment saying how everything's perfect, when that's obviously not the case? Yet that's essentially what we do when we play at faith while trying to avoid the spotlight of God's judgment. According to the Scripture above, we are not condemned because of our sin but because we cling to the shadows. Jesus Christ already paid the penalty for all sin for all people for all time. The toughest part has already been done. What remains is for each of us to trust that we can actually venture out of the darkness and into His light. To believe that when we step into that light, we won't be exposed and humiliated but cleansed and restored.

A counselor friend of mine once said, "Your mental health is as sick as your darkest secrets. And likewise, you grow steadily more healthy in direct proportion to the unveiling of those secrets." Imagine the freedom you would experience if you were fully known by God and those closest to you. We all long for intimacy in our relationships. One way that intimacy can be defined is "into-me-see." How have your attempts to keep others from knowing the real you destroyed rather than built intimacy?

Several years ago when Hanne and I were with another couple for dinner, the conversation went deeper than most. My friend Dave made a rather bold assertion: "I think most guys have things they believe they could never tell anyone." Hanne stepped up right away to say, "I don't think that's true. I could tell Scott anything. Do you think there are things you could never tell me, Scott?"

I hemmed and hawed for a while and finally said in a most definitive way, "Well, I don't know . . . maybe."

I wasn't looking forward to the ride home and being needled about what things I felt I must keep hidden and not bring into the light. Actually, Hanne never brought it up. I was the one who kept thinking about it. *Why are there things in my life that I don't think I could talk about even with my own wife?* I concluded that it was because of my fear of judgment.

At that time, I was meeting with another friend on a biweekly basis for breakfast. This friend was serving as a sort of a spiritual advisor during a time of transition in my life. The morning before we were to meet, I came across James 5:16 in my daily Bible reading:

"Confess your sins to each other and pray for each other so that you may be healed."

It seemed that God was opening up an opportunity for me to allow His light to shine into a place that I'd kept closed off and dark. With fear and trepidation I took a big risk and told my friend, "I feel there's something I need to tell you. It has nothing to do with you, and it goes a long way back, but I want to tell you anyway." All the while I was watching him for hints of embarrassment, shock, judgment. There were none.

When I finished, he said to me, "Scott, in the name of Jesus, I tell you, *you're forgiven*."

In that instant, I felt as if a ton of bricks had been lifted from my shoulders. And I never again struggled with feeling guilty, shameful or condemned about that issue. In fact, shortly after that experience, I told my wife about it. She responded: "It means a lot that you told me that, but I don't get why you didn't feel you could say it sooner."

God assures us that what is done in darkness will come into the light.[64] Fortunately, we have the option of choosing when things come into the light—both before Him and before others. The amazing part is that when things come into the light through our initiative, they lose their sting and shame. And the hidden place that threatened us with condemnation instead becomes a place of safety and security.—*SL*

A Conversation with God

Dear God, thank you so much for your invitation to come into the light. It's because of your acceptance and forgiveness that I can even begin to entertain such an invitation. Help me to fully embrace your forgiveness for things that took place in my past. Help me to once and for all forgive myself. Help me also to make it right with others where I can.

Making It Real

What areas of your life do you still feel reside in the darkness?

What would be involved in bringing these areas into the light before God and others?

What could be the benefits of doing this?

Think of a couple of trustworthy friends who might be open to meeting together on a weekly basis for an hour or so with the goal of having no secrets in your lives. Take the risk today of beginning to intentionally order your life around authentic relationships where people know the real you.

For Further Exploration

For more help in finding healing in areas of shame, read Lewis Smedes's *Shame and Grace: Healing the Shame We Don't Deserve* (San Francisco: HarperSanFrancisco, 1994). A helpful book on establishing a small group for accountability and spiritual growth is Neil Cole's *Cultivating a Life for God* (Carol Stream, IL: ChurchSmart Resources, 1999).

Isn't All This Stuff About the Holy Spirit Just a Little Spooky?

I believe in the **Holy Spirit** . . .

> *[He] will ignite the kingdom life, a fire, the Holy Spirit within you, changing you from the inside out.*[65]
> —JOHN THE BAPTIST, SPEAKING OF JESUS

One evening, toward the end of my first trip to China, I wandered the streets of Chengdu, trying to find the best place to entrust the remaining 40 of the more than 600 Chinese Bibles and booklets we had smuggled in for the underground church.

Just the evening before, the head of our group had been arrested, and we knew that our window of opportunity was closing. At any time we might be arrested, and our "contraband" confiscated.

As I walked down a busy street, I was silently asking the Holy Spirit to guide me. I had never really spoken much to the Holy Spirit before, but somehow in these circumstances, speaking and listening to Him was more than just something to try on; it felt necessary to my survival.

During my brief time in China, I had learned to pay attention to those whom I was naturally drawn to, because they often seemed to know that we had something for them. One woman even told me that she had seen us in a dream and knew that we were going to bring Bibles to them. (I find myself hesitating as I write this, for it sounds strange to me now, though it was very natural in that context.)

On this occasion, I noticed a man watching me as he walked with his son, so I handed him a few small booklets. As I did so, a crowd began to gather around us. Sensing that at least one of those people did not have good intentions, I moved swiftly across the street. Two men from the group followed me. I walked faster, and so did they. Suddenly, all of the streetlights went out on that side of the street, and I ducked into a crowd of people along the road. It seemed that Someone else was guiding my steps, though it was unlike anything I had experienced growing up in rural Minnesota.

I quickly turned down an alley filled with small shops and darted inside a one-room store. The owner whisked me into a back room. Turns out he was a

Christian and connected with the underground church!

We couldn't speak each other's language, but that didn't seem to dampen our ability to communicate. I gratefully gave him the remaining Bibles I was carrying.

I stayed in that shop for nearly an hour before heading back to my hotel. I remember walking down the street in the misting rain at about midnight thinking, *Wow, I want to live like this every day. I feel like this is how life was meant to be. I wonder if it's how Jesus felt when He walked on Earth, allowing Himself to be guided by the Father, through the Holy Spirit.*

I felt such an intimacy with God, and the Holy Spirit seemed like my closest friend. I knew that it was just as possible to live this way back home, and I was determined to do so.

But of course it's much more difficult to deliberately depend on God when you are living in self-sufficient middle-class America. Apart from an occasional crisis, little of my life is lived really believing in—fully relying on—the Holy Spirit's power and guidance. Yet I desperately long to live that way.

Does that mean I have to live on the brink of death or destruction to really experience God? No. But I've discovered that nurturing an intimate relationship with Him does require some things from me.

First, I've noticed that I have to be intentionally

aware of the presence of the Holy Spirit. He's always there—closer than a brother or sister, as the Scripture says[66]—but if I'm not mindful of His presence, I won't even notice Him, let alone call upon Him.

And second, I must be willing to step out and act on the guidance that I sense the Holy Spirit is impressing on me, like releasing the grudge I've been nursing for so long and seeking reconciliation or making a phone call to the guy whose name keeps mysteriously popping up in my mind. It requires that I train myself to listen to that faint little voice. You know the one. You can recognize it when your natural response is "Oh, my. But if I did that. . . ."

This is where following through really takes faith and dependence upon the Holy Spirit. And it's where you find Him showing up and causing great things to happen—miracles even. And you say, "Wow, I want to live like this every day!"—*SL*

A Conversation with God

Dear Holy Spirit, I want to experience you today.
I want to become much more familiar with who you
are, to learn to hear your voice and to call upon you
for power to move where I sense you leading me.
I thank you that I don't have to look far to find you,
since you're as close as my own thoughts.

Making It Real

If you can, describe a time when you felt the Holy Spirit working in your life. How did you respond?

Are you at all uncomfortable around talk of the Holy Spirit? Why do you suppose that is?

In what ways do you believe that relying more fully on the Holy Spirit could make a difference? With that in mind, what step of faith will you take today?

For Further Exploration

For an inspiring look at how God is miraculously moving in places like China today, read the autobiography of Brother Yun, written with Paul Hattaway, titled *The Heavenly Man: The Remarkable True Story of Chinese Christian Brother Yun* (Grand Rapids, MI: Monarch Books, 2002).

Can't We All Just Get Along?

I believe in . . . **the holy catholic church** . . .

Each of us finds our meaning and function as a part of his body. But as a chopped-off finger or cut-off toe we wouldn't amount to much, would we? [67]

—THE APOSTLE PAUL

When I was a child, I would sometimes hear my mother and father argue. They would usually wait until after we were in bed to hash out their "big stuff." They didn't want my brother or me to hear. We did.

Sometimes I would sit up trying to listen, afraid of what I might hear. I remember crying, even praying, "I hope they can work this out. Please. . . ." Unfortunately, the threats of leaving and divorce eventually became reality.

My parents divorced when I was 16 years old. It felt unnatural and wrong for my family to be "split," sort of like losing a leg. God didn't design families to be split apart any more than He designed our bodies to lose limbs. In each case, the victim may survive the tragedy, but not without a noticeable limp.

In a similar way, the church is limping. God's people are a family that has suffered through divorce. His church is a body that has been severed. We have divided into factions, camps. The "divorces" exist not just between denominations and churches but within them. Some days I even wonder if we will survive the trauma of our many splits.

Does it ever bother you that the very people whom you would think should get along the best often can't—or won't—get along at all? Religious people in general, and church folks in particular, have filled history books and headlines with divisions, factions and even wars over God.

Isn't love the essence of our faith? Didn't Jesus command us to "love your neighbor as yourself"?[68] For a group that is supposed to be unified as the "holy catholic church," we are alarmingly divided.[69]

One might be tempted to (cynically) write a newer version of this phrase in the Creed, something more like, "the unholy divided churches." But let's set aside our pessimism for a moment and consider a few reasons why we should not indulge this temptation.

First, we should expect unity to be extremely hard work. Our idealistic notions about how the church "should be" might benefit from a little dose of reality. Few things in this fallen world are as they should be, and while the church is God's chosen instrument of grace on this earth, it is peopled with flawed individuals who are still working out their faith. It's important to remember that much of our work as followers of Jesus is to make things better. We move against destructive powers, including division. This is just as true in the church as in any other part of life.

Think about your own family or work environment. Do you often find yourself in the midst of disagreements that take incredible effort to work through? Don't you sometimes find yourself arguing with a spouse or friend, only to realize that you don't even remember what you were initially fighting about? Emotions get the best of us. We speak before we think. The tendencies to retreat and withdraw ("Then they'll know how angry I am!") or attack and manipulate ("How dare they do or say such a thing to me!") can thrive unchecked. These roots of division reach down in all of us, not just those in the church.

Second, unity requires more than simply pointing out areas of division. It's a good start to diagnose problems of disunity within our communities of faith, but it takes wisdom and skill to get on with the real work of engaging in loving actions that create, maintain and restore unity. Second-guessing how other people are managing (or mismanaging) conflict is much easier than actually stepping into the community yourself as a peacemaker. Some of the skills I have in mind are things such as good listening, gentle and loving confrontation, and the art of conflict resolution.

Finally, a unified church—a holy catholic one—is well worth the effort. A whole body is a strong body, a healthy one.

I've seen this firsthand. Earlier, I mentioned that my parents divorced when I was 16. As with all children of divorce, I'm sure that this has shaped me in ways I may never fully know. But something else happened after that, something that continues to shape me even more profoundly.

A few years after my parents' divorce, in the interest of giving their marriage a second try, my family started attending a little church in New England. Our experience there was refreshing, but I wasn't sure why. Looking back, I see that this small congregation offered a community of faith that was not divided, not lost in bickering and meaningless arguments. I am so glad that it wasn't an unholy divided body, but a unified one, getting along in its mission to be a blessing to the world.

Just by visiting this church, our family became beneficiaries of their unity. We were blessed by God through it. It was there, among God's family, that my family was reunified. My mother and father married each other for a second time, in no small part because of that "holy catholic church." They have been married, and a part of a church, ever since.

Good things happen when the church takes unity to heart and works hard at being the body.—*CM*

A Conversation with God

Dear Father, I see the damage that division causes, not only to the church, your body, but even to my own family, my own friendships. Will you help me to learn the wisdom and work of unity? Sometimes I want to attack people; other times I want to just run away. Help me to stay, to be a peacemaker rather than a second-guesser. I pray that you would use me not merely to point out the divisions in your church but to help heal them.

Making It Real

As you consider your own church experience, when have you fallen into the trap of only pointing out the conflict without doing the work of unifying?

How well do you listen to those with whom you disagree? Are you able to gently and lovingly confront someone?

What steps could you take to become a person who unifies rather than divides, not only in the church but also at work or at home? (Who knows, maybe the first step is a simple, old-fashioned apology.)

For Further Exploration

For a refreshing perspective on Christian theology and what unifies the church, read Brian McLaren's *A Generous Orthodoxy* (Grand Rapids, MI: Zondervan Publishing House, 2004).

What Does Community Have to Do with Church?

The whole congregation of believers was united as one—one heart, one mind! They didn't even claim ownership of their own possessions. No one said, "That's mine; you can't have it." They shared everything. The apostles gave powerful witness to the resurrection of the Master Jesus, and grace was on all of them.[70]

—LUKE, DESCRIBING THE CHURCH

At a Bible discussion group in a juvenile detention center, I asked the dozen or so boys in attendance how many were in a gang. Every hand went up.

"So why did you join a gang?" I then asked. I expected to hear disillusionment in their answers, like, "I joined a gang because I thought they'd always be there for me. But now I don't hear from anyone. No phone calls, no letters. Nothing. And one of my boys is hitting on my girl, even as we speak."

But what I actually heard turned my assumptions inside out.

Jason said, "I was looking for respect. I was a nobody when I joined my gang, but now everyone knows me. And I got respect."

Tyrone's answer was similar: "I used to be afraid to go out of the house at night in my neighborhood. Now nobody messes with me."

Tommy said, "I was looking for a place to belong, a place where I really matter."

Perhaps Edwin best captured the mind-set of the group: "I was looking for something big enough to live for and big enough to die for. That's what my gang gave me."

By this time I was ready to join a gang! They had described precisely the things I was looking for: respect, a place to belong, a purpose big enough to live and die for. Who wouldn't want that? Then I realized that I had a problem. We were all in agreement that gangs were the way to go—but that wasn't exactly the topic of the Bible study. How could I get out of this mess and lead them into something more redemptive?

"Let me read to you something about the first gang that I ever heard of," I said with a slight sense of desperation. The boys listened intently as I read the following passage from Acts 2:43-47:

> Everyone was filled with awe, and many wonders and miraculous signs were done by the apostles. All the believers were together and had everything in common. Selling their possessions and goods, they gave to anyone as he had need. Every day they continued to meet together in the temple courts. They broke bread in their homes and ate together with glad and sincere hearts, praising God and enjoying the favor of all the people. And the Lord added to their number daily those who were being saved.

When I finished, each boy remained quiet for a while. Finally, Jason commented, "Yo, that's real." After a few more moments of silence, he continued, "That's the church, huh?"

"Yeah," I said.

Another asked, "Do they have a church like that where I live?"

"I don't know," I confessed.

As I left that night, two things stuck out in my mind. First, each of these gang members resonated with the description of the early church given in Acts

2. It described exactly what they were seeking. Consider the definition of the Greek word for fellowship—*koinonia*—which is described in the above verses that I read to them from the book of Acts. It literally means: "to give, contribute, share. To be initiated into the mysteries of Christ. To participate in the deeds of others, being equally responsible for them."[71] A gang embodies the core definition of the term *koinonia*.

The second thought on my mind was that I wasn't sure where my young friends could find such a place.

Perhaps you have also felt dismayed by the gaping distance between what the church is called to be and what your experience of it has been. The words "hypocrisy" and "superficiality" frequently crop up during my conversations with people who have given up on church. These words also seem to pepper our excuses for the constant church-shopping we do when we're in the consumer mind-set of trying to find just the right church that will meet our needs without requiring too much of an investment from us.

Of course, no church is perfect; each one is made up of imperfect people like us. But how can we move closer to that authentic *koinonia* we all crave, that sense of true connection?

Perhaps it starts by recognizing that church isn't a building or a liturgy or a combination of music and message that moves our hearts. Church is about communion, something we create when we choose to come together in Christ's name to meet others at their point of need. Jesus said it best:

> Here is a simple, rule-of-thumb guide for behavior: Ask yourself what you want people to do for you, then grab the initiative and do it for them. Add up God's Law and Prophets and this is what you get.[72]

Looking at it from this standpoint, our deepest longings can actually be what bring us together—not just to have our longings met but to do for others what we so crave for ourselves. Mysteriously, we find our own needs met as we meet the needs of others. Our longing isn't simply for a relief from circumstances, but for a connection to something greater. When we serve as the hands of Jesus, touching those who need love, and as the feet of Jesus, carrying a cup of cold water in His name, we find a place to belong. We become a part of something greater than we could ever accomplish on our own. And who wouldn't respect that?

When we choose to invest in, give to and love whomever God has provided for us to be with in the moment, rather than waiting for someone to do that for us, authentic fellowship—true communion—happens.

The kids in that juvenile jail seemed to grasp the beauty of communion at a gut level. When we met the next week, I told them I'd been thinking about our discussion. I admitted that I didn't know of a church that focused on gang kids in the city that most of them came from, but I knew a pastor who was interested in becoming a church like that—if they were willing to help him.

"He wants *us* to help him?!" one boy responded.

"Yes, he said he's been praying for someone like you guys. He said nobody knows gang kids like you, and if you were willing to help him start a youth church one night a week in their building, he thinks it could make a big difference."

"Sure, I'd love to do that," they all chimed in.

It felt really good that night. Like how church should feel. Maybe that's because what we were doing—working together to lay a foundation for true community—is what church is all about.—*SL*

A Conversation with God

I happened to have a copy of the prayer of St. Francis in my Bible that night. I made some copies for my gang-member friends, and we all read it together to close out the evening. I invite you to pray it as well, right now, aloud.

Lord, make me an instrument of your peace.
Where there is hatred, let me sow love;
where there is injury, pardon;
where there is doubt, faith;
where there is despair, hope;
where there is darkness, light;
and where there is sadness, joy.

O Divine Master, grant that I may not so
much seek to be consoled as to console;
to be understood as to understand;
to be loved as to love.

For it is in giving that we receive;
it is in pardoning that we are pardoned;
and it is in dying that we are born to eternal life.

Making It Real

If you were to label what you most crave in your life right now, what would that be?

What if God actually placed that yearning in your life so that you could more effectively reach out to someone else who may be feeling the same need? Be specific about what you will do today to create authentic communion.

For Further Exploration

Great insights on how to become an authentic community and a positive influence in any church can be found in Larry Crabb's *The Safest Place on Earth: Where People Connect and Are Forever Changed* (Nashville, TN: Word Publishing, 1999).

Who Are These Saints
I Keep Hearing About?

I believe in . . . the communion of **saints** . . .

And I pray that you, being rooted and established
in love, may have power, together with all the saints,
to grasp how wide and long and high and deep is
the love of Christ, and to know this love that
surpasses knowledge—that you may be filled to
the measure of all the fullness of God.[73]

—THE APOSTLE PAUL

If you asked a group of people what makes someone a saint, you'd probably get a wide variety of answers. But the Bible uses the term simply to describe a follower of Jesus Christ.

Um, excuse me. That would make me a saint. I don't think so. And if you don't believe me, just ask my spouse.

It's especially difficult to envision God calling me a saint when I consider the fact that He knows everything about me: everything about my past . . . what I'm now involved in and thinking about . . . even my plans for the future. Everything. So I'm thinking He must be pretty disappointed with what He knows and sees. I'm not exactly what you'd call "saint material."

In fact, I'd venture to say that very few people would like me if they knew *everything* about me. And I'm talking about my flawed fellow human beings. What must a holy, perfect God think when He looks at my life, my heart, my thoughts?

And what about when He looks at you?

What if Jesus were to walk into your room right now? What do you think He would say to you?

Would He be disappointed? Would He be upset about your lack of spiritual depth? Do you think He'd be angry about all the sin you're still wrapped up in?

Would He lecture you? Would He pinpoint all of your flaws and remark on how you're messing up your life? Would He comment on your need to trust Him more?

Do you think He'd call you a hypocrite? After all, you say you're a Christian, but much of the time your words and actions don't show it.

You know what? Jesus could say those things to every Christian alive! But take a look in the Bible at how

He talked to imperfect, messed-up, self-centered people just like you and me. As I look at the stories of His life, I think Jesus would be much more likely to wrap His arms around you and say something like this: "You know, I love you so much. Last night while you were sleeping, I must have thought about you a million times. I just couldn't get you off my mind. I know your struggles, and I hurt with you. I just want you to know that I'm here."

Consider what the Bible says about how God sees us:

How precious it is, Lord, to realize that you are thinking about me constantly! I can't even count how many times a day your thoughts turn towards me. And when I waken in the morning, you are still thinking of me![74]

The LORD your God is with you, he is mighty to save. He will take great delight in you, he will quiet you with his love, he will rejoice over you with singing.[75]

Do you have a place in your mind for that kind of God—a God who knows you completely and yet loves you that much? A God who rejoices over you with singing, as the verse above says? A God who not only loves you but also likes you? He does. He really does!

"How can that be?" you might ask. "He knows all my sin and failures." But that's the whole point of why Jesus died on the cross: to pay for our sins and failures. Because of that, you are completely clean and accepted in God's sight. And rather than being a slave to your old ways, He has given you His power to do what is right.

Does that mean you'll never mess up again? No. We all get things wrong, over and over and over. But know and believe this: God is still on your side! He's not mad or fed up with you. He stands there waiting to embrace you and encourage you. So confess every sin. Ask for His forgiveness, accept it, and forgive yourself.

Then get on with the incredible life of being a saint.—*SL*

A Conversation with God

Dear God, thank you for your love for me. It's a love that is total, absolute, unreserved, unconditional, unfailing and constant. Thank you that you have accepted me completely. Help me to see myself more and more as you see me. And to act more in keeping with the way you see me: worthy of your great love.

Making It Real

Describe how you think God sees you right now. Explain the reasons behind your answer.

Based on what you saw in today's reading, make a new list of all the positive ways He feels toward you.

For Further Exploration

For an in-depth theological look at our completeness in Christ, read Miles J. Stanford's small but powerful *The Green Letters: Principles of Spiritual Growth* (Grand Rapids, MI: Zondervan Publishing House, 1985).

Are You Saying I Have to Forgive Everyone?!

I believe in . . . the **forgiveness** of sins . . .

Forgive the things you are holding against one another.
Forgive, just as the Lord forgave you. [76]

—THE APOSTLE PAUL

Watching the Mel Gibson movie *The Passion of the Christ* was a difficult experience for me. Like many, I found it exhausting to watch the two hours of relentless torture. Yet what I found perhaps most disturbing was the ending. After all the brutality He has endured, Jesus said from the cross: "Father, forgive them, for they do not know what they are doing." [77]

Where is the justice in that? Does every wrong done on Earth have to wait until eternity to be righted? And if this is the standard for Christians to live by, it seems pretty milquetoast to me.

My reaction might be blamed, at least in part, on the bitterness I was personally feeling at the time regarding the pain I was suffering at the hand of another person.

I was in the midst of building a major case for revenge when I went to the movie that night. I'm not talking about revenge in the sense of causing bodily harm—although that thought had crossed my mind more than a few times—but just getting even for what that person had done to me. At most I'd maybe expose his dark side, discredit his reputation, make him wish he'd never tangled with me—small stuff like that.

The last thing I wanted to think about was forgiving that person.

I had expected to feel somewhat consoled by going to *The Passion of the Christ*, believing it would highlight how small my pain was in comparison to what Jesus suffered. That did happen, but then came that annoying line: "Father, forgive them, for they do not know what they are doing."

That grated on me. Yes, they did know what they were doing, just as this man knows exactly what he's doing to me. And he needs to pay for that.

A couple days later, I came upon these words of Jesus in my daily Scripture reading:

Here's another old saying that deserves a second look: "Eye for eye, tooth for tooth." Is that going to get us anywhere? Here's what I propose: "Don't hit back at all." If someone strikes you, stand there and take it. If someone drags you into court and sues for the shirt off your back, giftwrap your best coat and make a present of it. And if someone takes unfair advantage of you, use the occasion to practice the servant life. No more tit-for-tat stuff. Live generously.[78]

Ouch.

Live generously, huh? As I thought about my life during the past several months, I could see how anger and revenge had moved into my mind and taken up residence, rent-free. And in the process, love, forgiveness and generosity had been evicted. It has been said that bitterness and unforgiveness is like preparing a cup of poison for your enemy, and then drinking it yourself. That was pretty much the case for me.

I began to pray that God would grant me a generous and forgiving attitude toward this individual—one that more accurately reflected the grace and forgiveness that God had extended to me. It started with the discipline of praying for him on a daily basis, of asking God to bless him. I must admit that my words felt more than a little inauthentic in the beginning, but I kept on praying that way as an act of faith.

Before long, my heart began to shift as well. I could see that this person was actually not free in what he was doing to me. He was held in bondage by his own fears. For who would ever do such evil in awareness? The ability to do evil or to be evil is not freedom but bondage. For those who are truly free cannot sin, just as God cannot sin.[79] Now I had a choice: would I live in freedom or in bondage?

Holding that perspective made a big difference. I could imagine Jesus on the cross, saying, in effect, "Father, please don't hold these actions against these people. They're so enslaved and trapped in their own fears and hurts and ignorance. They actually believe that what they're doing is right; but if they really knew the truth of who I am, they would never do this. Please don't hold it against them. Forgive them, Father."

By taking on a similar posture, I was able to engage with the person I had held so much resentment toward. Does this mean that I must forget what happened or put myself in the vulnerable position of trusting him again? No. Trust has to do with the future. Forgiveness has to do with the past. Does it mean I have to excuse what happened or say it's okay? No. I acknowledge what happened and that it hurt me greatly. But I'm no longer willing to allow that hurt to determine my future.

And because of how forgiveness is freeing me from the past, I'm able to enter the future with an entirely different attitude.—*SL*

A Conversation with God

Dear God, show me those areas of hurt and unfor-giveness that I am still holding on to: where my mind drifts to fantasize about revenge; where bitter-ness has taken root and is sapping the creative ener-gy and love from me. I lay this situation—this per-son—before you right now. Please give me a desire to forgive and then the courage to do it. Thank you for all you have forgiven me for. It far outweighs what I'm holding against this person.

Making It Real

On a piece of paper, record an offense you're still hold-ing on to in some form. Be very specific about it. Include the time, place and details of what happened and how it has hurt and affected you. Now crumple up the paper and hold it in your hands. As an act of faith, open your hands, releasing this person and situation into God's hands. As you do this, ask for His help to begin the process of forgiving this person, and thank Him for His help. Then either burn the paper or put it in the trash, determining never to hold on to the offense again.

Do you know anyone who is particularly forgiving or who has forgiven an awful hurt? Consider learning from them, almost as a forgiveness apprentice, the wisdom and art of making things right after they have gone so wrong.

For Further Exploration

An excellent and practical book on forgiveness is Lewis Smedes's *Forgive and Forget: Healing the Hurts We Don't Deserve* (San Francisco: HarperSanFrancisco, 1984).

Do We Have to Use the Word "Sin"?

And it's clear enough, isn't it, that we're sinners, every one of us, in the same sinking boat with everybody else? [80]

—THE APOSTLE PAUL

A young mother recently asked me if the people who taught children in our congregation about God would use the word "sin" when they taught. She said, "I'd hate for my children to feel so afraid of God and ashamed of themselves as I did when I was a child learning about sin."

I'd hate for her children to feel that way too. So I asked her, "What words would you prefer we use?"

Without hesitation, she said, "'Right' and 'wrong'. That's what we say at home. They just seem better to me. They don't have all that guilt loaded on them."

"When we talk about sin," I assured her, "which is really another way of saying 'wrong' and 'right', we don't add any guilt or shame or condemnation to it. As a matter of fact, we always infuse that discussion with love and grace. God's not against sin just because we're bad or because He's out to get us. He's against sin because it's bad for us and He is out to protect us. How does that sound?"

"That sounds much better," she sighed in relief.

Words are funny things, aren't they? A particular word catches our eye or sounds in our ear and, before we know it, our mind has painted a picture. Feelings start to flow. Attached and related thoughts pop up, along with other concepts that are connected in ways we can't quite explain.

The unanticipated impact of words presents a particular problem in writing a book that talks about God and spiritual matters. It's filled with words that are supposed to represent significant, even ultimate, realities—words like "believe," "forgive," "father," "love," "spirit," "sin," "heaven" and "hell." If you hope to make your message clear, you have to spend time addressing the misuse of such terms before you can even begin looking at what they were originally intended to communicate.

Consider that young mother and the word "sin." Just the mention of the word takes her back to when she was seven years old, and without any warning a full fare of shame and condemnation is served up.

But what does the word "sin" really mean? One way to think of it is, "to miss the mark."[81] In that sense, it's not much different than what this thoughtful mother is trying to teach her children at home.

On the other hand, it may be quite different, depending on what she's using as her measure of right and wrong. How we judge whether or not we've missed the mark hinges on what we consider that mark to be. Many of us live life sort of shooting arrows as best we can, and then drawing circles around those arrows and declaring, "Bull's-eye!"

But God measures our words and actions against His standard, not ours. And His mark is higher than any of us can reach. That puts us all on equal footing. No insiders and outsiders. No good people versus bad.

As Alexander Solzhenitsyn said, "The universal dividing line between good and evil . . . divides the heart of every man."[82] That's what the term "sin" portrays. You might be a step or two closer to the target than I am, but when we're gazing at a mark several miles away, the infinitesimal distance between us pales in comparison to our common condition of falling far short.

That's the bad news. The Creed, however, is about good news. Notice where the word "sin" is located: smack dab in the middle between the words "forgiveness" and "resurrection."

Consider what God has to say about sin and His remedy for it:

> Since we've compiled this long and sorry record as sinners . . . and proved that we are utterly incapable of living the glorious lives God wills for us, God did it for us. Out of sheer generosity he put us in right standing with himself. A pure gift. He got us out of the mess we're in and restored us to where he always wanted us to be. And he did it by means of Jesus Christ. God sacrificed Jesus on the altar of the world to clear that world of sin. Having faith in him sets us in the clear.[83]

Sometimes you have to acknowledge the bad news before you can embrace the good news. Are you ready today to concede how far you are from hitting the mark—and to accept God's willingness to close the gap for you?—*SL & CM*

A Conversation with God

God, I readily admit to you that I am a sinner.
I've fallen far short of the mark. Please forgive me
for all of my sins. Thank you for making a way
for me to know you and to be rightly related to you,
forever. I'm placing my trust in you and
what you have done.

Making It Real

What do you feel when you hear the word "sin"?

What does this reveal about your proximity to the bull's-eye of what's truly "right"? What does this reveal about your relationship with God?

For Further Exploration

For more on how to believe in Jesus, check out Brian McLaren's *Finding Faith: A Self-Discovery Guide for Your Spiritual Quest* (Grand Rapids, MI: Zondervan Publishing House, 2001).

Is There Really Life Beyond This One?

I believe in . . . **the resurrection** of the body . . .

> *Everybody dies in Adam; everybody comes alive in Christ.*[84]
>
> —THE APOSTLE PAUL

The first time I saw an actual dead body, I was about five years old. Completely terrified, I gripped my mother's hand as I knelt next to the body of my deceased great uncle during a wake.

I was puzzled as to why they called it "a wake" when my great uncle looked just the opposite. Then, as I gazed a little longer, I saw his chest move a little. And then his finger twitched. Well, maybe not. I wasn't really sure either way.

I wondered, *Is he really dead? Is that really my uncle?* Some of my aunts leaned over and kissed him. *What are they doing?! What does he feel like?* Finally, when I was sure no one was looking, I quickly touched his hand. I will never forget how it felt: a little like a stone, though not as hard or cold. But lifeless and utterly unnatural.

Seeing a body void of life is strange, if not terrifying, especially for a five-year-old. Yet death, painful and foreign as it seems, is an inevitable part of life, and it waits somewhere "out there" for every one of us.

The Apostles' Creed touches on the topic of death and where it fits in our lives—or perhaps more accurately, just how unfitting it is to the way things were meant to be. The word "resurrection" confirms that death is real but it is not forever. Death is not the final word.

Of course, that is a statement of faith. Some scoff at the idea that death leads to something beyond this life. One friend said to me, "When we're dead, we're dead. That's it. It's over." Of course, that's *also* a statement of faith. My friend can't prove to me that he is right, any more than I can prove to him the truth of my beliefs. We both have faith, just in different things.

Sometimes I think my belief that there is a resurrection—and that death is not the end—is more of a stretch than his. After all, I haven't personally seen someone come back to life. He, on the other hand, has seen many people die with no evidence that any of them were resurrected. I must confess, I'm often tempted to think this way too, assuming my personal experience to be the sole evidence for truth.

But then I think about Jesus being resurrected. I believe that He was, not just because I want to, but because of evidence that goes far beyond what I have personally seen.

Evidence? Yes. What else could explain the dramatic change in His disciples? These backbiting, betraying wimps who ran away in fear when Jesus was arrested transformed almost overnight into death-defying martyrs after they saw that He had been raised from the dead. Or how about the fact that even non-Christian historians of Jesus' day, like Josephus, refer to Jesus' resurrection? Scores of books have been written validating the resurrection of Christ historically. All of this and more offers good reasons for our heads to believe.

But what about our hearts?

When we ponder death as a reality, our hearts rebel. The Resurrection reminds us that death does not really fit into life. And in the end, it will not have the last word. When we face the death of loved ones, the resurrection reminds us that in Christ our relationship with them isn't really over. The separation is temporary. When we face our own mortality, the resurrection inspires us to trust and hope that God is not done with us. We will *rise again*.

Since that first time when, as a little boy, I saw death close up, I have seen it many times. I've witnessed relatives, friends and even children lying lifeless in a coffin. My head remembers Jesus and His resurrection. Each time, as I kneel next to them and pray, I think to myself, *This cannot be the end.* And my heart, moved to remember the many promises of Scripture, reverberates with the assurance, "It is not."

In some strange way, the roots of my hope in God grow deeper one death at a time, because both my head and my heart agree: it's not over when we die.

I believe in the resurrection. . . . —CM

A Conversation with God

Dear God, hoping in something beyond this life sometimes feels foolish to me. Death is such an ugly enemy. Help me to trust that you hate death as much as I do, maybe even more. Help me to understand, as best I can, that you will somehow, some way, someday, embrace us in Christ beyond our death. Help me to believe, not only with my heart but also with my head, that death is dead and we will rise again.

Making It Real

Think of the last time you attended services for a loved one who had died. Did you find yourself hoping in something beyond death?

How different would grief be for you if you believed that in Christ, we will rise from our deaths?

Take some time this week to ask a friend or two what they believe about death and about resurrection. Don't be surprised if the conversation is short or awkward (or both), because talking about death is difficult for many of us. Try anyway. It will help you sort out why you believe what you believe about death and resurrection.

For Further Exploration

For more on evidence of Christ's resurrection, read Lee Strobel's *The Case for Christ: A Journalist's Personal Investigation of the Evidence for Jesus* (Grand Rapids, MI: Zondervan Publishing House, 1998) and Josh McDowell's *Evidence That Demands a Verdict* (San Bernardino, CA: Here's Life Publishers, 1979).

Does God Do "Extreme Makeovers"?

I believe in . . . the resurrection **of the body** . . .

Some skeptic is sure to ask, "Show me how resurrection works. Give me a diagram; draw me a picture. What does this 'resurrection body' look like?" [85]

—THE APOSTLE PAUL

To our dismay, the vast majority of us share the experience of being on a diet. I'm sure there are many reasons we go through the often torturous experience of attempting to lose weight, but the Creed sheds light on something that many people overlook about Christian faith: It affirms that our bodies matter.

I have a friend who, to use her words, has an "issue" with beaches. She refuses to go because she is so ashamed of her body. She is mortified by the thought of being "exposed." As she talks, you get the sense that she's ashamed not just of her body, but of her*self*. From her perspective, she's not just *in* her body, she *is* her body. Part of me wishes that she would separate her identity from her physical state. But from my own experience, I know how hard—how nearly impossible—that is.

Something in each of us longs to live in a strong, healthy, vibrant body. That something is at least partly God-given. After He made us, God looked over His creation and said, "It was so good, so very good!"[86] But though we may have appeared very good to God at the beginning, sin and evil in all their forms have done serious damage to our bodies. We are far from paradise.

Maybe that's why millions of us are glued to the so-called reality TV shows about people who become completely "made over." Their striving for perfection reflects our own desire for at least a little self-improvement.

Admittedly, some of this is vanity. Some of us would simply like to look better for the sake of feeling more attractive. But some of our longings include a plea for health, a yearning for a body free of disease or disability. Much of our desires regarding our bodies stem from the reality that we are, by God's design, bodily beings.

That's why the resurrection *of the body* is so important. Our bodies matter not only to us but to God as well. So much so that even though we may be separated from them for a time when we die, that separation is temporary. Our permanent and true home is in our bodies. And the reality of the resurrection means that we will be living as bodily beings forever.

Now I can imagine some people saying, "Are you kidding me? I don't want my body now, let alone forever! It hurts. I'm sick. I want one that works!" Others, like my beach-phobic friend, might say, "I just want a better one (thinner, stronger, taller . . .)." That's why it's reassuring to know that our current model isn't the permanent one.

In Paul's discussion on our bodies, he wrote, "We're only looking at pre-resurrection 'seeds'—who can imagine what the resurrection 'plants' will be like! . . . You could never guess what a tomato looks like by looking at a tomato seed."[87] One thing's for sure: Our resurrected bodies will be radically different from our present ones.

We will still have bodies. They will be ours. They will even somehow get their origin from our current ones. But our new bodies will be beyond anything we can even imagine now. Beaches won't be an issue for anyone. Neither will wheelchairs, braces or hospitals.

If it is true that our bodies—in whatever future form they may take—will be reunited with our souls and that we will live within them forever, what does that have to do with our lives *now?*

Consider a few questions as you think about how our physical life and spiritual life intersect: Is it possible to think more "spiritually" about things such as eating well, exercising or other physical activities that enrich and strengthen our bodies? Understood from a "whole life" perspective, might these activities be just as spiritual as praying? Maybe one way to get our *spiritual* hearts pumping is to take a brisk walk to get our *physical* heart pumping.

But at the same time, wouldn't it be nice if we could help each other relax about having to be just the right (says who?) shape and size? God made us the way we are *and* He will remake us, perfectly. Our resurrection will be the most extreme makeover in all of history!—CM

A Conversation with God

Dear Father, please help me to be thankful for my body. Though I can't say I like everything about it, your design remains truly amazing. I can only imagine what my soul and body will be like someday. Things that are hard for me to imagine, like the

*resurrection, are also so hard for me to believe. Help
me to trust you on this. But also help me to take care
of the body that you have given to me now. Help me
to better care for it, as well as for my soul.*

Making It Real

This may seem awkward, but give it a try: Stand in
front of a mirror and look—really look—at the body
God gave you. Take an inventory from head to toe. Be
amazed at how well your body is designed for making
its way in this world. Consider the form and multiple
functions of each part—your eyes, legs, arms, ears, toes.
And though some parts may not work as well as you
might prefer, consider with gratitude what *does* work.
Thank God for your body. Then think of one way you
can strengthen or help it, treating it like the spiritual
gift that it is.

For Further Exploration

To learn more about the connection between healthy
living and healthy relationships, read Gary Smalley's
Food and Love (Wheaton, IL: Tyndale House Publishers,
2001).

Will Life Ever Be the Way It's Supposed to Be?

. . . and **the life everlasting**.

Compared to what's coming, living conditions around here seem like a stopover in an unfurnished shack, and we're tired of it! We've been given a glimpse of the real thing, our true home. . . . The Spirit of God whets our appetite by giving us a taste of what's ahead. He puts a little of heaven in our hearts so that we'll never settle for less.[88]

—THE APOSTLE PAUL

The other day I received a brochure in the mail from a travel agency. It posed the question, Why wait for heaven when you can lock in your week in paradise now?

This struck me as a great question. Why *should* I have to wait until the next life for things to be the way they're "supposed" to be?

I confess that I've bought into more than a few sales gimmicks in the hopes of securing a slice of heaven for myself in the here and now. But even in the midst of paradise vacations, I find myself left wanting.

It's rather disillusioning to discover that as good as this world is, it will never be all that my heart yearns for. But then, who wants to live in an illusion anyway? Ultimately, says the Scripture, we've been created for another place. This world is not our home.[89] After all, why would God put such longings in our hearts if there wasn't a way—ultimately—for them to be satisfied? Maybe that's what Paul meant when he said of the Holy Spirit, "he puts a little of heaven in our hearts so we'll never settle for less."[90]

What comes to mind when you think of heaven? I must confess that I tend to imagine a bunch of really nice people doing lots of really nice things, being really careful not to offend or get in the way of anyone else. And there's lots of singing. And it will all last for a really, really long time.

That all sounds, well, really nice, but not terribly exciting or inviting.

So I'm sort of caught between loving it here yet living with the reality that this life will never fulfill the deepest longings of my heart—and not feeling particularly excited about life on the other side.

And sometimes I feel guilty about that. Like I really should be a lot more excited about heaven. My hesitancy probably has to do with the fact that it's almost impossible to imagine what it must be like there. We just don't have much to compare it against.

It's a bit like trying to describe life on the outside to a baby still in her mother's womb. We could say, "We can't wait for you to come out here. You're gonna love it! There are beautiful trees and sunshine and wonderful people who will love you."

"What's a *tree*?" she would likely ask. "What's a *sunshine*? What's a *people*? And what's *love*? I like it in here where it's dark and warm, where I can eat 24/7 and always hear my mom's heartbeat. Is it like that out there?"

"Well, uh, no. But—"

"Well, then I'm not interested. I'm going to stay here."

It would be hard to describe something so "other" to someone with such limited understanding, wouldn't it?

John must have struggled with that when he wrote the book of Revelation. He tried to describe in earthly terms the vision of heaven that God had given him, but he was bound by human language, experiences, concepts and images. Imagine the enormous challenge of searching for words to explain what he was seeing.

What did he come up with? A place of such beauty that it takes your breath away. It's a place where there are no tears, only overwhelming joy. It's a place where life is how it's supposed to be. John mentions things like gold and light, but you get the sense that he can't find words that even begin to describe what he saw. About the only thing we have to base our hope on is that God made this place called Earth in seven days, and He's been working on heaven ever since.[91]

But then, all of this talk of an afterlife is just a theoretical discussion—until we're confronted with the stark reality that life on Earth as we know it ends, for every one of us. We can try to ignore it, but we can't escape the reality of death.

Holding a focus on "the life everlasting" can give a different perspective to death, however, and that's what has made the difference for me.

We received an e-mail recently from an elderly woman that Hanne and I had met several years ago. Her words illustrate for me the richness that comes in living a life where death is a "comma" rather than a "period":

Dear Scott and Hanne,

Remember me? Lois Anderson. I'm Don's widow now since he slipped away into the Father's presence last Thursday afternoon. We are directing any donations to your ministry, as Don was so very burdened for troubled teens.

I'm still in the midst of reflecting on our wonderful life together. Quite honestly, we both had hoped the other would go first, so the one to remain wouldn't be faced with the difficulty of having to live alone.

While I miss him greatly, I'm so very glad for how he went. Here one minute and with the Lord the next. He went out to do some snow blowing, assuring me he would call me if he got tired. I opened the door again and he was lying on the cold pavement. I couldn't even comprehend it, as I had just talked to him not five minutes earlier. When I got to him, it was just his body. My sweetheart had already been rejoicing in heaven. And knowing that makes living so much easier for me, too.

In His great love,
Lois

Something about knowing that one day things will all turn out the way they're supposed to allows us to engage more fully in today—making life here just a bit more like it's ultimately supposed to be.—*SL*

A Conversation with God

Dear God, thank you that as your child I'm going to live with you in heaven, forever. I don't know what it will be like. But I know that it will be so much greater than all the best this earth has to offer. Thank you also for the assurance that one day everything will work out as it's meant to be. In the meantime, give me the courage to influence the world around me to be a little more like heaven here on Earth.

Making It Real

What do you think heaven will be like?

If you really believed that death was a comma instead of a period, how might that change the way you live?

For Further Exploration

An excellent book on the quest for eternal meaning is Donald Miller's *Searching for God Knows What* (Nashville, TN: Thomas Nelson Publishers, 2004).

How Can I Keep Hanging On to Faith?

Amen.

The grace of the Master Jesus be with all of you. Oh, Yes! [92]

—JOHN, PRAYING THE FINAL VERSE OF SCRIPTURE

During an out-of-town business trip, I called home to talk with my family. As the conversation wound down and we all began to say our good-byes, my daughter, who was about seven at the time, said, "Okay, Daddy, amen! Oops, I mean good-bye!" We got a kick out of her slip. But it started me thinking about how that little word "amen" has sort of lost its punch.

Because we have heard it so often, nearly always in the same way, we lose the sense of what "amen" actually *means*. We tend to use it as if we were saying good-bye to God, sort of like a religious version of "over and out."

Instead of serving as a signoff, amen is actually a word of affirmation and agreement. You may have noticed in the Scripture above that the translator says, "Oh, Yes!" rather than "Amen," at the end of the prayer. That captures the grand spirit of this small word. When someone says, "Amen!" he or she is casting a vote of faith in the words previously spoken.

Rather than saying, "Okay, I'm done praying now," saying amen is a way of saying, "Okay, I'm ready to trust now." Amen represents faith language, which is why the Apostles' Creed closes with it. Amen gives the Creed a tone of prayer rather than of doctrine.

As we have made our way through all of these statements of faith in the Creed, amen declares our intention to trust to the best of our abilities that these things are true—and to live accordingly. We are ex-pressing and even celebrating our faith *in* God, *to* God and *with* each other.

Saying amen is a little like nodding our heads as we listen to others. Their words resonate within us. We agree. We may not understand everything they are saying, but even then, we give them the benefit of the doubt. Healthy and humble faith does this with God. We give Him the benefit of our doubts.

Our faith, if it's real, connects somehow to the world we live in, helping us navigate through our broken and fall-en reality. Faith, too, can be broken, or even lost. Amen reflects our commitment to hold on to our faith, even when it's broken. To search for it even when it feels lost.

The first baptism I performed as a student-pastor was for the newborn daughter of close friends. When she died in the first month of her life, the faith I had claimed before confronting this tragedy withered. But in retrospect, I see how that was largely a faith of theory, of tidy answers and neatly organized doctrines, all of which looked great in a book or a classroom, but frankly sounded silly in a pediatric intensive care ward. I had placed God in a box, as the saying goes. That box was buried with that little girl.

In truth, I didn't really *lose faith;* I lost *my* faith. I didn't stop believing; I started believing differently. A new faith grew out of the old one. My itsy-bitsy "I-think-I-can-understand-most-of-what-I-need-to-know" faith died. Out of the old faith rose a new one that was more genuine, although at times less explainable. And that process is still continuing today.

For skeptics, authentic faith placed in a good and strong God can be fragile while we are living in a painful and unfair world. I get tempted, like many people, to get stuck asking why. Faith often doesn't find answers to that question.

But we can still say amen, nodding with God, if we are willing to look past what we can't know to the things that we can. As we allow our faith to grow, it often involves letting go of our desire to always have answers. But we never face our questions of pain or evil without *Him*. We are not alone. He is too good and strong to leave us alone.

Has your heart begun, even slightly, to nod in faith, saying amen with parts of this creed? Are you feeling ready to express your faith in the loving, wise and powerful God revealed within it? As you continue to listen for Him, our prayer is that you will also grow in your trust of Him. The payoff is well worth the risk!

Amen.—*CM*

A Conversation with God

Write out the Creed from page 24 as a prayer. Feel free to intersperse personal words of gratitude and declaration as you write.

Making It Real

This step on your journey of faith is over. We hope that you are more curious, more interested and more motivated to keep searching and seeking. It's time to take the next step. Read through the Gospel of Mark and start learning more about your Father almighty, His Son and the Holy Spirit. Try to connect with some friends who are on the same journey, maybe the person who gave you this book or invited you to church. Most important, be prepared for God to be true to His promise that when you seek, you *will* find Him.

For Further Exploration

Other books that reveal how daily situations point to deeper spiritual truths—and that might serve as good follow-up reading to this book—are Donald Miller's *Blue like Jazz: Nonreligious Thoughts on Christian Spirituality* (Nashville, TN: Thomas Nelson Publishers, 2003); Anne Lamott's *Traveling Mercies: Some Thoughts on Faith* (New York: Pantheon Books, 1999); and The Monks of New Skete's *Rise Up with a Listening Heart* (New York: Yorkville Press, 2004).

The grace of the Master Jesus be with all of you. Oh, Yes!
Amen.

Endnotes

1. Richard Rohr, *Everything Belongs: The Gift of Contemplative Prayer* (New York: Crossroad Publishing Company, 2003), pp. 45-46.
2. Proverbs 8:17, *THE MESSAGE*.
3. *The American Heritage Dictionary*, 2nd College Edition, s.v. "skepticism."
4. Luke 11:9-10, *THE MESSAGE*.
5. The Apostles' Creed, translation of the Latin text as approved by Christian Reformed Church in North America.
6. Mark 4:24.
7. Anthony De Mello, *The Way to Love* (New York: Doubleday, 1991), p. 47.
8. Philippians 1:21.
9. Philippians 1:12-14, *THE MESSAGE*.
10. Mark 9:24.
11. The Barna Group, "American Faith Is Diverse, as Shown Among Five Faith-Based Segments," *The Barna Update*, January 29, 2002. http://www.barna.org/FlexPage.aspx?Page=BarnaUpdate&BarnaUpdateID=105 (accessed May 2005).
12. Augustus Gordon, quoted in Brennan Manning, *Ruthless Trust: A Ragamuffin's Path to God* (San Francisco: Harper-SanFrancisco, 2000), p. 4.
13. 2 Corinthians 5:7.
14. Hebrews 11:1, emphasis added.
15. Manning, *Ruthless Trust: A Ragamuffin's Path to God*, p. 5.
16. Rueben P. Job and Norman Shawchuck, *A Guide to Prayer* (Nashville, TN: The Upper Room, 1983), p. 374.
17. Isaiah 40:18,28, *THE MESSAGE*.
18. Matthew 6:9.
19. Matthew 7:9-11, *THE MESSAGE*.
20. Mark 15:36.
21. R. Laird Harris, Gleason L. Archer and Bruce K. Waltke, *Theological Wordbook of the Old Testament*, (Chicago: Moody Press, 2001), no. 310b.
22. 2 Corinthians 12:10, *TLB*.
23. Genesis 1:26, *THE MESSAGE*.
24. Genesis 1:27-28,31, *THE MESSAGE*.
25. See Genesis 1:27-28.
26. Matthew 16:15, *THE MESSAGE*.
27. Donald Palmer, *Kierkegaard* (New York: Writers and Readers Publishing, 1996), p. 65.
28. John 6:68-69, *THE MESSAGE*.
29. Jim Elliot, *The Journals of Jim Elliot,* ed. Elisabeth Elliot (Old Tappan,

NJ: Revell, 1978), p. 174. Online version at http://www.wheaton.edu/bgc/archives/faq/20.htm.

30. Matthew 3:16-17, *THE MESSAGE*.

31. For some, thinking of God as one being yet three persons is an obstacle to taking the Christian faith seriously. I don't want to ignore this intellectual obstacle. However, God is beyond the capacity of our finite minds to fully comprehend, so wouldn't we expect that many aspects of His nature would be difficult to understand? Mysteries, like the exact nature of the Trinity, are simply part of the deal when it comes to God.

32. Mark 8:34, *THE MESSAGE*.

33. Mark 8:34-37, *THE MESSAGE*.

34. W. E. Vine, Merrill F. Unger and William White, Jr., *An Expository of Dictionary Biblical Words* (Nashville, TN: Thomas Nelson Publishers, 1984), p. 308, s.v. "discipleship."

35. Luke 1:37, *THE MESSAGE*.

36. Dictionary.com, s.v. "miracle." http://dictionary.reference.com/search?q=miracle.

37. Luke 1:35, *THE MESSAGE*.

38. Hebrews 11:1, *THE MESSAGE*.

39. John 1:14, *THE MESSAGE*.

40. Philippians 2:7-8, *THE MESSAGE*.

41. Hebrews 2:17-18; 4:15, *TLB*.

42. See Philippians 3:10.

43. Hebrews 2:14-15, *THE MESSAGE*.

44. Martin Doblmeier, *Bonhoeffer* (Alexandria, VA: Journey Films, 2003), movie.

45. 1 Corinthians 15:55.

46. 2 Corinthians 5:21.

47. 2 Corinthians 5:17.

48. Merrill F. Unger, *Unger's Bible Dictionary* (Chicago: Moody Press, 1966), p. 520, s.v. "impute."

49. Psalm 139:8,11-12.

50. See 2 Peter 3:9.

51. Matthew 5:3, *THE MESSAGE*.

52. Luke 22:42.

53. Ephesians 1:19-20, *TLB*.

54. John 12:24-25, *THE MESSAGE*.

55. Mark 16:19, *THE MESSAGE*.

56. John 14:3, *THE MESSAGE*.

57. Colossians 3:2, *THE MESSAGE*.

58. Romans 8:33-34, *THE MESSAGE*.

59. John Ortberg, *Love Beyond Reason* (Grand Rapids, MI: Zondervan

Publishing House, 1998), pp. 166-167.

60. Romans 8:34, *THE MESSAGE*.

61. See 1 Corinthians 15:19,25-26.

62. Romans 8:38-39, *THE MESSAGE*.

63. John 3:19, *NRSV*.

64. See 1 Corinthians 4:5; Job 12:22.

65. Luke 3:16, *THE MESSAGE*.

66. Proverbs 18:24; John 15:15.

67. Romans 12:5, *THE MESSAGE*.

68. Mark 12:31

69. The word "catholic" refers to the unified nature of the universal church, not to a certain denomination.

70. Acts 4:32-33, *THE MESSAGE*.

71. Walter Bauer, *A Greek-English Lexicon of the New Testament and Other Early Christian Literature*, 2nd edition, revised by William F. Arndt and F. Wilbur Gingrich (Chicago: University of Chicago Press, 1979), p. 438, s.v. "*koinonia*."

72. Matthew 7:12, *THE MESSAGE*.

73. Ephesians 3:17-19.

74. Psalm 139:17-18, *TLB*.

75. Zephaniah 3:17.

76. Colossians 3:13, *NIRV*.

77. Luke 23:34.

78. Matthew 5:38-42, *THE MESSAGE*.

79. Anthony De Mello, *The Way to Love*, p. 39. See also John 8:32-36 and 2 Corinthians 3:17.

80. Romans 3:19, *THE MESSAGE*.

81. Vine, Unger and White, Jr., *An Expository of Dictionary Biblical Words*, p. 1045, s.v. "sin."

82. Alexander Solzhenitsyn, quoted in "Alexander Solzhenitsyn: Repentance and Moral Renewal," Russian-American Christian University, February 1998. http://www. racu.org/context/reflect_feb1998.html (accessed May 2005).

83. Romans 3:23-25, *THE MESSAGE*.

84. 1 Corinthians 15:22, *THE MESSAGE*.

85. 1 Corinthians 15:35, *THE MESSAGE*.

86. Genesis 1:31, *THE MESSAGE*.

87. 1 Corinthians 15:40,37, *THE MESSAGE*.

88. 2 Corinthians 5:4-5, *THE MESSAGE*.

89. See 2 Corinthians 5:1-2.

90. 2 Corinthians 5:5, *THE MESSAGE*.

91. See John 14:2-3.

92. Revelation 22:21, *THE MESSAGE*.

Reading for Your Next Step in Your Spiritual Journey

What the Bible Is All About
Bible Handbook, *NIV* Edition
Henrietta C. Mears
ISBN 08307.30850
***KJV* Edition**
ISBN 08307.30869

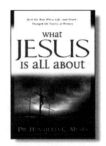

What Jesus Is All About
Meet the Man Whose Life—and Death—
Changed the Course of History
Henrietta C. Mears
ISBN 08307.33272

Soul Survivor
Finding Passion and Purpose
in the Dry Places
Mike Pilavachi
ISBN 08307.33248

So What's the Difference?
A Look at 20 Worldwide Faiths
and Religions and How They
Compare to Christianity
Fritz Ridenour
ISBN 08307.18982

Also Available from Regal

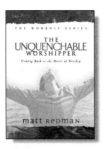

The Unquenchable Worshipper
Coming Back to the Heart of Worship
Matt Redman
ISBN 08307.29135

The Heart of Worship Files
Featuring Contributions from Some
of Today's Most Experienced
Lead Worshippers
Matt Redman, General Editor
ISBN 08307.32616

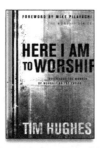

Here I Am to Worship
Never Lose the Wonder
of Worshiping the Savior
Tim Hughes
ISBN 08307.33221

Facedown
When You Face Up to God's Glory, You
Find Yourself Facedown in Worship
Matt Redman
ISBN 08307.32462

Also Available from Regal

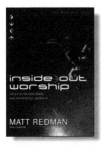

Inside, Out Worship
Insights for Passionate and
Purposeful Worship
Matt Redman and *Friends*
ISBN 08307.37103

For the Audience of One
Worshiping the One and Only
in Everything You Do
Mike Pilavachi
ISBN 08307.37049

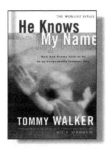

He Knows My Name
How God Knows Each of Us in
an Unspeakably Intimate Way
Tommy Walker
ISBN 08307.36360

The Worship God Is Seeking
An Exploration of Worship
and the Kingdom of God
David Ruis
ISBN 08307.36921